The
EXCEPTIONAL
LIFE

Books by Stephen Arterburn

FROM BETHANY HOUSE PUBLISHERS

*Regret-Fee Living**
*Midlife Manual for Men**

BEING CHRISTIAN*
Being Christian
Being Christian Workbook
Being Christian Group Leader's Kit
Being Christian DVD and CD-ROM Pack

*with John Shore

The
EXCEPTIONAL
LIFE

8 POWERFUL STEPS
TO EXPERIENCING GOD'S BEST FOR YOU

STEPHEN
ARTERBURN

BETHANY HOUSE PUBLISHERS

a division of Baker Publishing Group
Minneapolis, Minnesota

Published by Bethany House Publishers
11400 Hampshire Avenue South
Bloomington, Minnesota 55438
www.bethanyhouse.com

Bethany House Publishers is a division of
Baker Publishing Group, Grand Rapids, Michigan

Printed in the United States of America

Library of Congress Cataloging-in-Publication Data
Arterburn, Stephen.
    The exceptional life : 8 powerful steps to experiencing God's best for you / Stephen Arterburn.
        p.   cm.
    Summary: "The book presents eight issues that hold people back such as guilt, shame, fear, anger, and isolation and helps readers replace them with positives such as hope, love, trust, forgiveness, connection and community"—Provided by publisher.
    ISBN 978-0-7642-0425-8 (hardcover : alk. paper)
    1. Christian life. 2. Change—Religious aspects—Christianity. I. Title.
BV4509.5.A759 2011
241'.4—dc22   2011025205

Cover design by Lookout Design, Inc.

Author is represented by WordServe Literary Group

11 12 13 14 15 16 17   7 6 5 4 3 2 1

To Kenny. You have lived it.

Contents

Acknowledgments

My thanks to Kyle Duncan and Christopher Soderstrom for their exceptional work.

John Shore, my writing partner, is a genius. If you read anything in this book that is good or pretty good, it came from me. If you read something that is genius, it came from John. This book is the fourth work of mine that contains a John Shore brain implant. The books are much better because of John, and I am a much better person due to John's influence. Thank you, John Shore.

Introduction

The other day in my small group I was asked a very personal question. Everyone was invited to answer; I wasn't being singled out. The question was, "What makes you cry?"

There are lots of things that make me cry, and more often out of joy than out of sorrow. So I talked about my propensity to weep, just like my father did, at the drop of a hat.

It isn't anything I'm particularly proud to admit, but the truth is I'm a pretty emotional guy. Not that I get all weepy watching TV soaps, like my grandfather did. But certain songs bring a tear to my eye whenever I hear them. And I tend to think about my own feelings, and the feelings of other people, a whole lot more than I think about the kinds of things that maybe people who *don't* think about feelings think about: linear equations or investment ideas or sporting events.

What registers with me, personally—what sticks with me, what I notice the most, what I'm growing more sensitive to—are feelings. Emotions. Passions. Hurt. Need. Love. My whole life is centered around relating to and dealing with people and their feelings. And I've had to work through and overcome some pretty tough feelings myself.

Now that I am older, what I hear, in a word, is *hearts*. I'm more about matters of the heart than about anything else. It's a very good thing I am that way, too. Because while my heart is busy intaking and processing all kinds of input and information, my mind has ADHD. If my heart was as bad at sticking to one thing as my mind is, I'd be in serious trouble.

I do sometimes miss an appointment or find myself standing in the middle of a store wondering what it is I'm supposed to be buying. I might forget where I put my car keys (or, as happened just recently, my car); I might not tie my shoes; I might even board a plane I thought was going to one place, only to arrive in another. Honestly, stuff like that happens a lot. That's just life with ADHD.

Last week, when my wife, Misty, and I returned from small group, Mary Kaye was at the house watching our kids. There was a knock at the door; it was a group member returning my Bible, which I'd forgotten. Misty said to Mary Kaye, "He does this kind of thing all the time."

Ten minutes later there was another knock. It was the group leader returning my wife's purse, which *she* had left behind. It was a great moment for me!

Anyway, I don't have any trouble whatsoever paying attention when a person is talking to me about something that really matters to her. Then I'm 100 percent *there*.

If someone's sharing a problem he's having—an upsetting recent conflict, struggles and failures with an addiction, or anything causing general or specific emotional stress—then I tune in to him like a ham radio beside a ten-thousand-watt transmitting tower. (It's not like I know *nothing* about technical stuff. Sure, I've no idea what a transmitting tower is, and I wouldn't know a ham radio from a ham sandwich. But I *sounded* like I knew what I was talking about, didn't I? That's about half the battle right there.)

What's good for me is that my profession is perfectly suited to my nature. For my radio and TV program, *New Life Live,* I spend hours at a time listening to people share their deepest, most personal issues. And that's just while we're doing the show. In addition, I give seminars and lectures and engage in the New Life weekend retreats for healing for those who are fighting depression, anger, addiction, relationship problems, and every kind of thing you can imagine that ever blocks a person from experiencing God's best.

Listening to people is what I love doing. With my heart, I listen to theirs.

Guess what, though? Turns out that for all these years my mind *has*, in fact, been paying attention to what my heart's been doing. While my heart has been intensely focused on the troubles, concerns, and challenges of tens if not hundreds of thousands of others, my mind—ADHD and all—has been watching and tracking what's going on between my heart and each and every one of those people.

The reason I know this? About a year ago, my mind started niggling me to write down a note or two about something it was trying to tell me. So I started making sure that (insofar as I was capable) I was never without my trusty pad and pen.

Here's what I discovered: after years of intimate exposure to others' sufferings, my mind had discerned *patterns* in why and how people tend to become, to varying degrees, dysfunctional. I had slowly but surely come to the realization that no matter what the *manifested* problems of any given individual might be—whatever stood between themselves and God's best for them—the *root* of their issue almost always boiled down to the same thing: they were hanging on to something they needed to let go of, or something was hanging on to them that needed to be knocked off.

Let me say that again: *hanging on to something they needed to let go of.*

In almost every single person I've ever counseled, something they're clinging to is preventing them from getting to something much better.

There's been, in other words, something they needed to give up, in exchange for which they'd get more than anything they ever could have envisioned.

"Good job, mind!" I said. (Since I was in my neighborhood coffee shop at the time, I said it to myself. At least, I hope I did.) "You've done it. You've boiled down the things people clutch, the things they need to give up so they can receive something much better, to eight things! I'm so proud of you. I now officially forgive you for all the times you've driven off with the gas-pump hose still attached to the car and made me pay for damages on the spot."

Eight things. I believe that if I were to take the main problem anyone's having in life, no matter what it is—no matter how severely it's interfering with their own well-being or that of those around them—I'd be able to boil it down to the fact that they must release one of eight things in order to gain for themselves the beneficial qualities that hanging on to this one thing is preventing them from owning.

1. Any person can give up guilt and shame, in order to get back hope.
2. Any person can give up resentment, in order to get back love.
3. Any person can give up fear, in order to get back trust.
4. Any person can give up anger, in order to get back forgiveness.
5. Any person can give up instant gratification, in order to get back patience.
6. Any person can give up learned helplessness, in order to get back power.
7. Any person can give up isolation, in order to get back connection and community.
8. Any person can give up addiction, in order to get back freedom.

And there it is: you relinquish one bad thing to gain one very, very good thing. That's what this book is about. You could say it's about upgrading your life from mundane to exceptional.

Each chapter of *The Exceptional Life* deals with one of the give-up-to-gain relationships listed above. Within each chapter, you'll find five sections.

The first section is about making sure you're perfectly clear on the nature of one negative quality—on what exactly that chapter is helping you give up. We'll identify the must-go quality: we'll isolate its features, delineate its nature, talk about its origin.

The second section will look at the negative impacts of that quality, at how the possesion of that thing completely undermines all that's positive and healthy about your life.

The third section will offer practical, psychological, and spiritual, Bible-based advice on how to finally, once and for all, give up the negative quality.

The fourth section will discuss the healthy, God-centered positivity you're certain to gain as a result of banishing what was blocking you from it.

The fifth section will present what discovering and possessing this newfound godliness will do for you. Here we'll talk about exactly how you can be sure that, from then on, your life will improve in ways you might not have dreamed possible.

Finally, we'll conclude with several questions to stimulate group discussion about the chapter's content.

In summary, each chapter breaks down into

1. what needs to be given up;
2. why it needs to be given up;
3. how to go about giving it up;
4. what you'll gain from God in giving it up; and
5. what you'll be able to do and be once you've given it up (*plus* some great discussion topics).

So there you have it.
Want to upgrade to the Exceptional Life?
Let's get started.

1

Give Up Guilt and Shame; Get Back Hope

(1) What Are Guilt and Shame?

Fallen and human

Adam and Eve *were* living the Exceptional Life. Literally, it was all good. But just like today, for so many with so much, it was not enough.

> She saw that the tree was beautiful and its fruit looked delicious, and she wanted the wisdom it would give her. So she took some of the fruit and ate it. Then she gave some to her husband, who was with her, and he ate it, too. At that moment their eyes were opened, and they suddenly felt shame at their nakedness. So they sewed fig leaves together to cover themselves. . . .
>
> Then the Lord God called to the man, "Where are you?" He replied, "I heard you walking in the garden, so I hid. I was afraid because I was naked."
>
> —Genesis 3:6–7, 9–10

It's pretty easy to forget that shame and guilt are now part of the human condition. And each has its own unique reasons to exist. God doesn't intend for us to be stuck, though, in an inner world that only hauls us down or pushes us backward. Instead, what God wants from his fallen flock is "godly sorrow."

Godly sorrow leads to repentance, to change, to good action. Godly sorrow is a key to transformation. It's a big part of God's plan for us.

We all know what happens to the person who begins to believe he's just as good as God—that he's just as pure and right and capable. Those are the most lethal things a person can begin to think about himself. So God has built it into the very core of our characters that we *not* feel that way.

In this sense, what we feel when we sin—the godly sorrow that's part of God's redemptive plan for humankind—is an experience that protects us from the damage of hubris. We don't want to have the wrong kind of pride in ourselves; *that's* sure to begin for us a long, long fall, all the way back down to the point where we remember that God, after all, is in charge of everything.

And we must remember this. We must remember: this is God's world; we are God's children; our fate and well-being—indeed, not just of our lives but the lives of everyone else and of the world itself—are in God's hands.

Let's start with the reasons you might feel *guilt*. And actually, there are only two.

First, if you feel guilt, then you're involved in a sin, repeating a sin, or choosing to sin. (See also "Second," immediately below.)

If all you feel is guilt, then all you feel is bad, and feeling bad does not help you change your behavior. In fact, one way to feel better, though ineffectively and only temporarily, is to repeat your sin of choice and experience the immediate gratification that comes from it.

We all sin. We're all imperfect. But some of us are so caught up in a sin that you could say the sin owns us and controls us—it's destroying us by breaking our connection with God and with those who love us.

18

Second, the other reason for feeling guilt: maybe, for example, after doing wrong, you've repented, turned the other way (changed), and asked God to forgive you . . . but the guilt *still* is nagging you. If that's the case, then, at least for your own personal sin, you either don't fully believe, have not accepted, or have even rejected God's forgiveness, the complete divine forgiveness made possible through the blood Jesus Christ shed to redeem you.

When I was in college, I paid for an abortion. I certainly felt guilt once I realized what I'd done. However, I persisted and, therefore, existed in silence without anyone knowing my sin. The guilt didn't motivate me to change—it simply cut me off from the rest of the world.

I was a Christian, and I thought I'd gone too far, sinned too badly, to be forgiven. So I stayed stuck in my self-obsession, which did no one any good. It took truth and love and grace to move me out of guilt and into godly sorrow. My life was then headed in a totally different direction.

The guilt was a sign that something was very wrong in my life. Your guilt is a red flag either to accept what Christ has done for you or to stop whatever sin you're doing.

Shame is different. Shame is an identity. Shame takes over every aspect and dimension of a person, sucks out her life, and compels her to carry on as "less than" or "one down from" everyone else.

Tragically, many people bear an unnatural burden of shame that should be someone else's. I've met hundreds of abuse victims who felt shame for what their abuser did. The abuser pushed his shame off onto the victim.

The blessed life—the abundant life—begins when we drop unwarranted shame and attain a new identity with a new direction.

The shame, for instance, that you got from your parents saying you were bad. Or the shame that's from the secret knowledge of the terrible thing you did, causing you to live in pain from the past. *That* shame is unnecessary; it's caustic to your life.

That's the shame we need to be rid of. And we can be.

19

Guilt and shame have no place staying in your life, and if either is in a holding pattern, you have some work to do, some choices to make that will free you and allow you to live vibrantly in God's grace and mercy and love.

Damaging yourself

If you take away the guilt that simply comes from being a part of that human state or condition the Bible tells us is "fallen," what you have left is the kind of guilt that's not connected to God in any way. Where there's no godly sorrow, a person's sense of wrong is purposeless. For instance, in some people, called sociopaths, there's no sufficient experience of wrongness. Where most of us would feel guilty, the sociopath often feels justified.

So the first kind of guilt—the kind brought about by the way God designed us—is good if we can feel it and then stop what we're doing (or start what we should be doing). The second kind—the kind caused by something we aren't still involved with—is very *not* good. It's flat-out bad. It robs us of hope, and we need to get rid of it (rather than ignoring it or rejecting it).

Whenever you lie, or cheat, or put selfish wants ahead of someone else, you're creating for yourself what I call *stagnate guilt*. And while I could spend a lot of words here talking about the kinds of things people do to bring about (and stay stuck in) such heart-stealing, mind-saturating guilt, I'm going to step onto a limb and guess that I don't need to. I'm going to guess that you're just about as familiar with what you do that causes you to live in stagnate guilt as you are of any other single item or issue in your life.

We're all that way. We all know what kinds of things we do that result in deep feelings of regret. We deceive. We steal. We have affairs. We put fleeting selfishness ahead of the very real needs of others. Time and time again we act in ways that we know are wrong, that we know are damaging to ourselves and others, that we know are displeasing to God.

Again, I'm talking about commissive, compulsive, self-destructive choices and actions we make and do because we're so out of touch with ourselves and with God that we feel powerless to stop and change. I'm talking about sins that own us, control us, and destroy us.

What happens when we choose those and do those? Once more, we don't *only* hurt others; I hurt me, and you hurt you.

In fact, my wrongdoing almost always hurts me more than it hurts the person I've wronged. Probably he will—and fairly soon—get over whatever it is I did. He'll likely just say, "I finally realize Steve Arterburn is a thoughtless, small-minded cretin. Good to know. Time to delete him from my contacts, unfriend him on Facebook, quit following him on Twitter."

But what surely will linger is the guilt I feel for doing what I did. It'll eat away at me, too. It'll depress me and make me turn on myself in all kinds of ways that will serve only to weaken my resolve to change. In the end, the guilt I bring on myself and then keep dragging around will sap me of my hope.

Judging yourself

It's a funny thing. Well, actually, it's not funny at all. But it is true that whenever people do a wrong thing, they often make that thing even worse—at least, worse for themselves—by then harshly judging themselves for doing it.

Let's say I was in the lunchroom of our New Life offices. (And I want to emphasize: this *fabricated example* never, ever really happened.) Let's say I noticed on the counter a box of donuts someone was cruel enough to bring. Let's furthermore say that, in idle curiosity, I lifted the lid. And let's say I saw inside the only remaining donut; let's call it . . . oh, I don't know . . . chocolate-glazed. And

21

let's *pretend* I love the chocolate-glazed ones so much I'd practically drive over a good friend to get to one.

Then, let's say that as I was staring at the delectable treat, I heard someone coming down the hallway. Envision me closing the lid, turning, and leaning back against the counter with the box directly behind me—hiding it from view, as it were.

"Any donuts left?" says the gal who walks through the door.

Before I can stop myself, I blurt, "There aren't. Too bad, isn't it?"

She leaves. I grab the snack, wrap it in a paper towel, hide that in the fold of a magazine, return to my cubicle, sit at my desk, open up the "package," and chow down on that bad boy like it's the last donut in the world.

Honestly, I haven't done this. But I've *thought* about doing it. And if I ever had, do you know what would've hurt me much more than superfluous calories, or the knowledge that I'd deprived someone of a fleeting pleasure?

Self-incrimination. That's what would have kept chewing on me long after I'd finished chewing. Plus, instead of apologizing to the person I'd deceived, I wouldn't, because then I'd be afraid of what she thought of me. How or why would she ever trust me again if she knew I'd lied to her just to acquire junk food?! The problem would get worse and worse inside my own head until it had basically paralyzed me.

We think we're good, or naturally adept, at discerning the motives and identifying the essence of success or failure in others. Most of us are. But what most of us are *really* good at is judging ourselves.

We tend not to give ourselves half the breaks we give others. We're our own harshest judge, without question. We say things to ourselves we'd *never* say to a friend or, maybe, to anyone.

That's a problem. Not only must we stop doing the things that keep hope-dissolving (stagnate) guilt hanging around, we also need to stop compounding the wrong by heaping on self-judgments that are out of whack with (and over the top of) the severity of the harm we did in the first place.

Oftentimes, all we need for starting on the path of freedom—back into hope—is to give ourselves a "Get Out of Jail" card. That card is a combination of God's grace and our responsible behavior.

(2) What Guilt/Shame Does to Your Life

Poisons your well

We've all heard it said that one bad apple can spoil the whole bunch. Though I believe that's true, I can't really vouch for it myself, because I don't buy apples in "bunches"; I buy them in a bag, usually four or five at a time.

I know for sure, though, from firsthand experience, that one bad strawberry eventually *will* spoil all the others in its container. There's just something about a strawberry deciding to grow a beard that inspires all the berries around it to do the same thing. Before you know it, the delicious fruit you were looking forward to having on your scoop of vanilla looks like a rabid baby rodent that would make you run screaming if you saw it coming toward you on the sidewalk.

That's just the way strawberries are. One turns, and it can spoil a carton.

Why do I mention this? Because guilt and shame are the fuzzy berry in the bushel that's your life. They ruin everything. And it doesn't take them much time, either.

I've brought home a box of perfect, beautiful strawberries, placed them on the counter, gone to and from the mailbox, put my things away, checked my messages, and then come back to the kitchen and, seemingly already, found my fruit transmogrified into a geriatric Chia Pet. Just like that, what could have been a wonderful, refreshing treat became *When Hairy Met Berry*.

Guilt and shame poison the way you perceive and respond to both yourself and everyone and everything else. They're a merciless team, caustically compromising the integrity of everything they infiltrate.

Guilt and shame are like the heavily tinted sunglasses you're tempted to put on whenever you're feeling particularly guilty and shameful. They don't darken some of the things you see while allowing you to see others in their natural light. They darken all.

Nothing looks good when you're intaking it through guilt and shame. Nothing looks okay. Nothing looks healthy. Everyone, everything is shaded and shadowy.

A person plagued by guilt or shame has genuine difficultly participating in life in any enjoyable way. She's prevented from fully engaging with others because she feels as though she has a yoke around her neck, blocks of cement strapped to her feet, a heavy load on her back. Where others see smiles, she sees pained grimaces. Where others experience laughter, she experiences forced or false happiness. Where others feel joy, she feels empty and vacant. And she just can't shake off the weight that's pinning her to the ground throughout what could be the best flight of her life.

Makes you feel unworthy of love

As I alluded to earlier, there was a shameful episode in my past, one I've written about and spoken about hundreds of times. During college, I got my girlfriend pregnant. When I found out she was with child, I pressured her into doing something now repugnant to me: persuading her to undergo an abortion.

One thing about that awful time, something on which I haven't written much at all, was how utterly unworthy of love the guilt and shame left me feeling. Doing something against the very order of nature ruins your ability to think of yourself as anyone whom anyone else could ever love. You feel that anytime anyone even looks at you, all they see is all you can see when you look in the mirror: your shame.

I remember, right after what I did, walking through the grounds of our school and seeing, everywhere, young people, my age, having what looked like the best of times. They were playing together on the lawns, sitting in groups and talking. Couples were walking hand in hand; buddies were joshing and jostling each other. Everyone just seemed in so much harmony with the others all around. And I felt like I had a disease, as though if you touched me your arm would fall off. Or as though if you looked at me you'd run off screaming, because you'd have seen a monster.

I felt I'd never again be part of any sort of loving relationship. I allowed guilt and shame to leave me believing I was beyond the reach of love, beyond the compassion of others, forever severed from all sentiment or affection.

How could anyone love me *now*? They couldn't. They wouldn't. I'd be alone, always.

Thankfully it didn't eventuate that way. Jesus would show me that even a miserable sinner could receive his love and accept his sacrifice that cleanses away all sin. Slowly but surely I began to emerge from the deep hole in which my thoughts and actions had buried me; with the help of Jesus—and the painful process of making amends and restitution—I was able to reclaim the sense that I, too, had a place in the sun.

Finally, I again took my place among the living. And I can tell you, I'm so grateful to be back in the thick of a good life every moment I'm in it.

But I've never forgotten what it was like to be outside of life, so blanketed by and consumed with guilt and shame that sometimes it seemed I could barely go on existing. If you're filled with guilt and/or shame to where you sometimes feel the same way, hang on. Take it from me: if you're willing, Jesus will see to it that you don't feel like this forever.

Makes you stuck in the past

I once knew an elderly man I'll call Tom. When Tom was about seventy, his wife of four decades, "Joan," passed away.

25

I knew them for years before Joan's death. When they were together, Tom wasn't someone you'd be quick to call the world's most loving husband. The hard truth of it is, he simply didn't treat Joan very well. He was quite dismissive of her, too quick to belittle or make fun of her; generally speaking, he tended to act like a jerk toward her. It wasn't pleasant to be around.

It was worse than just how he behaved toward Joan in public, too; about ten or so years into their marriage, Tom had a series of affairs, secretly at the time. In tears, Joan, much later, confessed to me that Tom had never really apologized. He'd ended the trysts, and he'd felt that should have been good enough for her. It wasn't, of course, but in the interest of maintaining the appearance of a relatively happy household, Joan had contented herself to pretend it was.

When she died, Tom went into a depression that, honestly, caught a lot of those who knew him by surprise. He seemed to love his wife more after she was gone than he had when she was alive.

As time went by, Tom, instead of gradually pulling out of the grief anyone feels after losing a spouse, seemed to feel worse and worse. And increasingly, the only thing he seemed capable of talking about was what an angel on earth Joan had been. He seemed almost obsessed with his memories of her, which, frankly, never seemed to match up well with the quality of time he actually did spend with her.

As I talked with Tom over the period of about a year, I began to realize what was happening. He felt so bad about how he'd treated Joan that his mind and consciousness wouldn't let him continue on with his life after his chance to correct his longstanding wrong had literally died. Almost as literally, he was getting stuck in the past.

You know what they say about a criminal always returning to the scene of the crime? He does so because he's looking for something valuable, something he left behind there: his conscience.

That's what Tom was doing. He was trying to find the peace he'd never cared about back when it would have been much easier to claim.

For a long time, Tom wasn't honest with himself about why he couldn't let go of what was causing him deep-down distress. He had to disguise, even from himself, the fact that much of why he was grieving over "angelic Joan" had less to do with the person Joan actually was and more to do with his own burden of guilt and shame over how he'd treated her when she was here.

With a lot of counseling and prayer, Tom eventually made his true peace with Joan and with the person he finally outgrew.

His process teaches a valuable lesson: as long as guilt and shame keep their grip on you, you *cannot* fully occupy the present, let alone prepare for the future.

(3) How to Give Up Guilt and Shame

Unload baggage that isn't yours

Getting free of guilt and shame isn't the easiest thing to do. In those two traps are many snares that catch your leg, grab at your coat, threaten to yank you back down. Chief among those challenges: learning to understand the difference between what you should feel guilty about and what you shouldn't.

At first, that seems so simple, doesn't it? If I get angry at someone and say something awful, then later, when I'm feeling guilt, it's easy to know exactly why. Such obvious, cause-and-effect guilt isn't a mystery to untangle.

But this isn't the kind of guilt that's so crippling to so many. If you struggle with feelings of guilt that rarely if ever truly "go away," then almost certainly, in your life, there's a deeper issue—a shame—that goes beneath what you can access immediately just by taking an inventory of how you've behaved. In your search for its cause, the digging must go deeper.

When you dig deeper, if you do so diligently and honestly, you're bound to find some things that surprise you. Mainly, you'll find that much of the shame that for a very long time you've been assuming just naturally belongs to you *doesn't*. It's not yours. You didn't cause it; you didn't bring it about.

You've been willing to believe you did something wrong; you've been willing to assume that a lot of the blame for whatever trouble has been with you was, in fact, based in what you once did or said, or didn't do or say. However, quite often that's actually not the case.

Frequently we've accepted moral responsibility for something going wrong that wasn't anything we could stop. Many people who've been victimized instead see their role as perpetrator. This common, human-nature propensity begins where all dysfunctional thoughts or feelings do: childhood.

For instance, if your mom yelled at you or hit you and pointed at you while saying "You're bad," you believed her. You didn't realize she was saying you'd *done* something bad. What you heard—what your young mind registered as indelibly true—is that *you* are bad. Inherently, intrinsically *bad*. That while other children are good, obeying their parents and never causing any grief, you caused yours nothing but pain.

Most such examples—the ones that involve most parents and most children—are far less overt. Misguided-but-wrong words and actions from parents toward kids often are implicit and, frequently, even unspoken. All the same, every medium for that message delivers the same damaging verdict.

Sure, as kids we did some bad things, and we didn't stop doing some bad things once we weren't children anymore. But there's a big difference between making some wrong choices or carrying out some bad actions (on one hand) and *being* bad, as a person (on the other).

If you ever find yourself lost in feelings of shame for which you can't find a definite reason, go back. Go back to your childhood. Go back to a time when you were very young, when you felt like what your parents were conveying to you—in one explicit way or in a hundred subtler ways—was that you, yourself, *are* bad.

28

Then, tell yourself you weren't bad at all: you were just a child.

Feel that burden lifting? That's you, unloading from your life and from your consciousness baggage that was never yours to begin with.

For far too many people, though, it's not so easy to lift shame's burden. They were victimized, from out of nowhere, by an abuser, whether someone familiar or unfamiliar. When the abuser puts his or her shame on the victim, the victim often carries it for years. And abuse can come in many forms.

I remember talking with a woman about the abortion she'd had at sixteen. She got pregnant, and her mother forced her to abort— marched her to the clinic and then watched it happen. The girl was riddled with shame for years.

When I heard this, I told her that she had not had an abortion. An abortion had been forced on her and performed on her, but the abortion was not of her doing. There was no reason for her shame.

Yes, she'd had sex with the guy, and that was wrong. But the abortion itself was something beyond her choice. She had been carrying her mother's shame for years; in fact, she'd really wanted to raise the baby herself.

Look more carefully at your "transgressions"

Without going into too many details, I once did something I knew I shouldn't have done, a not-terribly-significant transgression against a friend. But I did it anyway. And then felt bad about it. For a long time, too.

I was certain he was aware of what I'd done and, thus, was no longer very keen on remaining my friend. I definitely understood this; I wouldn't have wanted to be his friend if he'd done to me what I had done to him.

So, convinced that he no longer cared to associate with me, I let our friendship fade. As more and more time went by, I saw him less and less.

Finally, though, I wasn't comfortable with that. I'm not the sort of person who likes to leave emotional work undone, and I felt in this case that's exactly what I'd done. One day, even though we hadn't spoken in quite a while, I called and invited him out for coffee.

It was good to see him again; before long, we were chatting just the way we had back when we were closer.

At last, I got up the nerve to share why I'd asked him to meet with me. I apologized for the wrong I had visited upon him, and while my confession was sincere, I also explained all the conditions at work in my life at the time that had conspired to compel me to act in ways that had later caused me great guilt and shame.

Guess what? He didn't even know what I was talking about! The incident that in my mind had taken on so much importance that I'd allowed it to ruin a dear friendship was something about which the "victim" of my mendacity was scarcely aware.

Let me clarify: he had known what had happened; he'd been cognizant of the general circumstances surrounding the event that had led, basically, to my running away. But he hadn't blamed me for anything. He didn't hold me accountable for anything. As far as he was concerned, I'd let our relationship fade because I had moved on to other things, and other people.

Later, when I thought about it, I saw that, again, my "transgression" wasn't nearly as dramatic as it had seemed to me. Because of my respect and affection for my friend, I'd blown what I'd done out of proportion. I hadn't hurt him. I hadn't insulted him or shown him disrespect. He barely cared about what I had done; from his point of view, it was entirely understandable.

Just like that, I had my friend back. And I'd learned a big lesson: if something you've done to someone else is eating at you, revisit it. Examine it. Authentically, forthrightly talk it over with the other person. You really might find that she not only was unhurt by what you did but also never even saw it as an affront in the first place. At

30

the very least, she might forgive you. Isn't it worth restoring a broken relationship to try to find out?

Remember you're only human

A basic but important thing I sometimes say to people who call in to *New Life Live* is this: at some point it's critical to remember you're only human.

We expect so very much of ourselves. Most of us are more than willing to forgive others their transgressions . . . but when it comes to our own, we aren't quite as gracious or generous.

We want to be perfect. We want to be the best mother or father or husband or wife or sister or brother or employee or employer—and on and on and on—that we possibly can be. When we fall short of our self-expectations, we often turn to guilt or shame, which we then carry around and which only serve to make us even less effective than we surely would be, if only we took a moment, every now and then, to remember that we are, after all, *human.*

Not God. Not Jesus. Just us. Just fallen, mortal *us.*

Nowhere is the case for what it really means and feels to be human put forth more succinctly and eloquently than in Romans 7, where Paul says:

> The trouble is not with the law, for it is spiritual and good. The trouble is with me, for I am all too human, a slave to sin. I don't really understand myself, for I want to do what is right, but I don't do it. Instead, I do what I hate. But if I know that what I am doing is wrong, this shows that I agree that the law is good. So I am not the one doing wrong; it is sin living in me that does it.
>
> And I know that nothing good lives in me, that is, in my sinful nature. I want to do what is right, but I can't. I want to do what is good, but I don't. I don't want to do what is wrong, but I do it anyway. But if I do what I don't want to do, I am not really the one doing wrong; it is sin living in me that does it.

31

I have discovered this principle of life—that when I want to do what is right, I inevitably do what is wrong. I love God's law with all my heart. But there is another power within me that is at war with my mind. This power makes me a slave to the sin that is still within me. Oh, what a miserable person I am! Who will free me from this life that is dominated by sin and death? Thank God! The answer is in Jesus Christ our Lord. So you see how it is: In my mind I really want to obey God's law, but because of my sinful nature I am a slave to sin.

—Romans 7:14–25

That's honesty. And that's how honest we're to become with ourselves.

(4) Gaining Back Your Hope

Remembering the cross

When you're filled with so much guilt and shame you sometimes feel you can barely get yourself out of bed in the morning—much less lead a happy, productive life—what you're missing is *hope*. That's what guilt and shame do: they make you feel like hope is simply beyond your reach.

We never have hope for something we know is just hopeless. If I see a man trying to float a hot-air balloon, and I can see the balloon has a gaping tear, I won't have any hope at all that it's going to fly. I can watch the would-be navigator pumping air like crazy; I can watch him put on his goggles and calibrate his compass; I can watch him tie ballast bags onto the basket. And still I'll know that for all of his planning and effort, he might as well be home on his couch enjoying a lemonade and a movie.

He might really, truly, deeply want the balloon to fly. He may even wish he could fly himself, without a balloon. But wanting and wishing aren't the same as real, live, certifiable hope.

32

In his amazing *Man's Search for Meaning*, Victor Frankel writes of how, in the midst of unthinkable suffering under Hitler's Third Reich, he stayed hopeful by clinging to the vision of one day lecturing psychiatrists on survival in horrible conditions. His hope became reality, as he fulfilled his dream once he was out of the Nazi death camp.

Frankel also tells of another man, some of whose dreams came true by coincidence. So when this man dreamed of a date on which they all would be emancipated, he believed it to be true. He thrived, with hope as his elixir.

It turned out to be false hope, though, not grounded in reality. When the date came closer, and there was no evidence they were about to be set free, the man became very ill; the day after the date passed, he died of dysentery.

When people lose hope, they're prone to feeling they've lost *everything*.

When we're burdened by guilt and shame, we feel like that damaged balloon: flat, useless, dead on the ground. We can feel too riddled with flaws even to believe we can be sewn back up and refilled with life. When we don't fill up and get up and move on, all we can experience is how awful it feels to live without the one thing—hope—that, maybe above all, brings us joy and meaning.

When you're guilty and shameful, you have no hope.

And when you have no hope, you're desperate. A person without hope is a shell. We need hope to keep going; why go anywhere at all if you know that "there" won't be any better than the terrible place you're at already?

What's the only thing a truly desperate person can do if he wants to get up off the ground and start living the life of significance God wants for him?

That's right: *turn to God.*

When you're without hope, you must turn to the only source of real hope: Jesus Christ, who gave his life on the cross as a sacrifice, in

33

our place, so that none of us ever again would need to be paralyzed by hopelessness.

If you're feeling full of guilt and shame, stop everything you're doing, right now, and turn your full attention to God. He's waiting to hear from you.

Get away to a quiet place and ask God to be there with you. Then quietly listen for his voice, or wait to sense his direction. If you don't, yet, just keep coming back until you do. He wants to restore your hope, and he will.

Now, a lot of us might think this would be enough. But it isn't. You also need *people*.

God uses people. He wants us to wait for his voice, but he also wants others to hear our voice—for instance, in the form of confession. We need others for connection; the key to this is confession.

We're to confess our sins to each other in order for healing to be complete (James 5:16). Paul instructs us to confess with our mouths, not only to get away and spend time with God in a closet (Romans 10:9)—and I say this as a big advocate of experiencing God in a closet. You need people, and people need you, if you're to experience real hope and, increasingly, real life.

Accepting God's love for you

A friend of mine had the craziest cat. She was adorable (the cat): gray and white, with little white socks. The interesting thing was, even though she clearly loved getting strokes, she always managed to stay just beyond the hand of my friend, who was always more than willing to give affection.

We'd be at her house, chatting, and Whiskers (not her real name—which is a joke, see, because cats can't read) would jump onto the couch beside my friend. Invariably, she'd reach out to pet Whiskers. And at the moment just before contact, Whiskers would move exactly beyond the reach of her hand again. Then Whiskers would roll over in an "I can't *wait* to get petted!" sort of way, and/or have an expression that seemed to say, "What happened? Thought you wanted to pet me. Aren't we friends anymore? Don't you love me?"

So my friend would lean over just far enough to reach Whiskers once more. If you've ever owned a cat (or, should I say, if you've ever been owned by a cat), you know exactly what Whiskers would do. She'd move again, just far enough away to barely be touched, and not nearly close enough to be petted.

That's how so many of us act when it comes to receiving God's love. We say we want it; we even *feel* we want it. And we do; we *do* want to be covered and filled with the glorious healing power of God's precious love for us.

But when it comes to actually receiving it, we move just out of reach. We pull a Whiskers. Instead of just waiting, and accepting for ourselves the love we know God wants to give us, wants to share with us, wants us to accept from him, we play hard to get.

And when we do this because we're filled with guilt and shame, we're not playing at all, are we? Then we're moving just beyond God's reach because we feel unworthy of the hope he's always trying to extend to us.

If that's something you know you're doing—if you're always stepping just outside of welcoming God's love for you—stop. Don't do it anymore. Stay in one place. Ask God, again, to love you. Then prepare for the best strokes you've ever received in your whole life.

Hope awaits you. Merely ask for it, and then embrace it when it comes.

Knowing God's love is a full-length feature (not a snapshot)

When you work, as I do, in the ministry of encouraging others toward a closer, deeper, more fulfilling relationship with Christ, one thing you bump up against all the time is the common idea that being with Jesus happens in a moment. I don't know if it's the culture we live in, where so many are so used to getting so many needs met so quickly, or whether it's primarily part of human nature to want most everything as soon as we can get it (or both). But whatever "it" is, it's definitely there in us.

People want a quick fix, basically. And I understand this. I'm especially that way if I get a little bit of something I've wanted an awful lot. If I sit down to watch a show with my wife and kids, and Misty goes into the kitchen to make popcorn, I'll think to myself, *You know, a couple kernels will be just the thing as I sit here and enjoy this time together.* Then I'll sniff it, wafting through the air, and I'll think how good it smells and how I can't wait to have a taste.

I only want a very little, I'll tell myself. *Popcorn's pretty much empty calories. And if there's a lot of butter on it, then it's worse than empty calories—then it can be* bad *for you. So I'll have just a handful.*

Then Misty brings a nice big bowl out to the den. Our kids launch what's essentially a full-on attack.

I, being one of the two mature adults in the room, know better. I slowly reach over, take a few kernels, and pop them into my mouth one at a time.

Then, though, in the span of maybe four seconds, I have to take care not to injure my children as I lunge desperately for the snack tub.

I thought I only wanted a sample. Once I had that taste, I wanted it all.

With regard to God's love, wanting it all is a good thing. You should be ravenous for the love of Jesus Christ. At the same time, however, understand that, with God, there is no finish line. There's no "goal." There's no *enough.*

Unlike with popcorn (and I ought to know), with God there's no bottom of the bowl (or barrel). There's always—always—more.

Real hope in life doesn't come from fully knowing God all at once. Part of what you must learn to hope for is this: getting to know him, and his ways, a little bit more, every single day of your life here on earth.

(5) Living a Life Filled With Hope

The optimism of a guilt-free life

We all have lots of choices. One of the things about which Americans have the most choices—or, at least, one thing we have many options about—is what exactly it is that we want. We can have almost any material good we seek (especially if we're willing to work hard enough to obtain it); and no matter how relatively poor, and despite situations or circumstances, anyone definitely can have almost anything he wants spiritually or emotionally.

The question wise philosophers and sage theologians long have asked knowledge-seekers who come to them for direction is, "What do you want?"

What do you want? Have you ever really asked yourself?

To accumulate money? To achieve fame? To become the world's most popular person? To attain absolute political power, so that everyone on the entire planet must do everything you command?

What is it that you want?

Well, I've given this much thought; I'm neither famously wise nor renownedly sage, but I've spent a lot of time pondering it for myself and asking it of others. Know what decades of considering this query have led me to believe? *The number one thing people most want and need in life is hope.*

Without hope, you have nothing. No spirit. No verve. No sense of adventure. No fun. No motive to get up in the morning. No purpose. No reason to survive and work to discover and enjoy a better day, a better season, a better life.

When *do* you have hope? Reality-based, life-sustaining, enduring hope? When you get free of guilt and shame. *Then* the world is your oyster. (Except I don't actually like oysters. The world can be your corn dog with mustard!)

Hope. This is what you have to look forward to, once you've shaken off that behemoth backpack of guilt and shame and finally can be free to embrace life as God has always intended.

A big part of hope, too, is optimism. Optimism produces motivation; without motivation, hope dies along with the life God has in store for you.

With optimism, motivation, and hope? Then life is wonderful, full of endless opportunities just waiting for you and God to make of them whatever the two of you will.

The future, free of the past

I'd like to explore that last paragraph just a little bit more.

Whenever I think about what it means to live a life of hope in Jesus, these are a few of the verses that come to mind:

I am leaving you with a gift—peace of mind and heart. And the peace I give is a gift the world cannot give. So don't be troubled or afraid.

—John 14:27

This is my command—be strong and courageous! Do not be afraid or discouraged. For the Lord your God is with you wherever you go.

—Joshua 1:9

For the despondent, every day brings trouble;
for the happy heart, life is a continual feast.

—Proverbs 15:15

A continual feast! This is one of my favorite lines in the whole Bible. I don't know any better way to describe a life that, because it's not ruled or dominated by guilt and shame, is lived with the joyous, optimistic hope that only knowing and walking with Jesus can provide.

When I wake up in the morning, I don't want to think about the past. I don't want to mull over all the wrong and awful things I did when I was young. I don't even want to think about all the wrong and awful things I did yesterday! How's that going to help me?

God doesn't want me wallowing in past sins and regrets.

Instead, *God wants me to have faith in the change he's waiting for me to accept from him as my inheritance as one of his followers.*

God doesn't want me sour or sad. He doesn't want me walking around with a long face, complaining to everyone about how ghastly everything is, moaning about the world being a terrible place, or lamenting over how this or that person did me wrong.

No way! *God wants me to live a life that reflects the hope he's promised me through his son, Jesus Christ.*

"Rejoice in our confident hope," says Paul (Romans 12:12). When I turn toward God, away from guilt and shame, indeed I'm free to do exactly that.

I owe it to myself, my family, my friends, and my God to do nothing less.

The importance of restitution

Before we move on from this—giving up guilt and shame to get back hope—let me spend a minute talking about restitution.

I have a friend I'll call Zebediah (since I'm tired of using "Tom" and "Bill" all the time). Zeb owned a software development firm in Southern California. A few years back, a very large company offered Zeb a whole lot of money for his much smaller company, and he took it. All his years of hard work had paid off. He'd made it. He was living "the American dream."

There was only one real problem with the good fortune that had come Zeb's way. He had a partner in the business.

"Throckmorton" wasn't an equal partner, at least not in terms of actually owning half the business; he'd invested a fair amount of money, to be sure, but his real equity had to do with the blood and sweat he had poured into it. He believed in the quality of the product Zeb had brought him onboard to help develop and market, and he'd proven this with his tireless efforts toward the company's success.

Ultimately, Zeb and Throck had different visions. Zeb's idea basically was to grow the company until it got large enough to attract the kind of buyout offers it eventually did, while Throck wanted to keep them privately owned and grow the company as far as he and Zeb could together. Throck was confident that the longer they waited, the more they'd be worth. He was decidedly against ever selling it out "early."

Zebediah was aware of Throckmorton's convictions when he got the first big offer. He accepted it anyway, without mutual discussion. He knew this wasn't a fair thing to do, yet he felt he had no choice, insofar as he did know that Throck wouldn't approve the sale—and (though he had no real fear of it) he didn't want any interference with the deal's proceedings.

It *was* Zeb's company. He *did* have a right to sell it whenever he wanted, to whomever he wanted, for however much he wanted.

But he'd hurt his friend and partner. While Throck made a lot of money in the sale, he was wounded that Zeb essentially had sold out behind his back.

The two former partners didn't talk for years. Then Zeb, on my firm advice, finally went to Throck and offered a full, profuse, heartfelt apology. Also, he offered to help fund any new effort of Throck's that needed capital. And Throck could have complete control.

"I felt so much lighter after I did that," Zeb said afterward. "The guilt of what I'd done had weighed on me all those years. I wish I'd apologized as soon as I'd done it."

Don't let an old wrong you've done weigh on you one more moment. Pick up the phone. Write a letter. Send an e-mail. But if you've hurt somebody, and you know it—and they know you know it—don't waste another minute being burdened by it.

Make restitution. You owe it to the person you hurt; you owe it to yourself; and you owe it to the one who is, after all, the Prince of Peace.

If your offense includes a financial component, true freedom will come with full restitution. Peace of mind and restoration of a relationship absolutely are worth the cost of making things entirely right.

Questions for Discussion

1. What do you think about the challenge of distinguishing between guilt and shame? (That is, between [a] guilt that results from something you've done that's wrong and [b] shame someone else may have dumped upon you or shame you inappropriately dump on yourself.) Do you find it easy or difficult to see where legitimate guilt stops and damaging shame begins?

2. Do you believe you judge yourself harder than you do anyone else? If so, why, do you think? Do you feel other people judge you as harshly as you judge yourself? Why or why not?

3. Have you ever been so burdened by guilt or shame that you were truly depressed? What did you feel during that experience? How did you rise out of that depression?

4. What does it mean, in your life, to live with a sense of hope? How does your "sense of hope" manifest itself? What things (or kinds of things) compel you to let go of your grip on hope? What strengthens your hope?

5. Do you feel you have trouble fully accepting the love God has for you? If so, why?

6. If you were free of virtually all guilt and shame, what do you think you'd do with your life? How do you think doing it would feel? What sorts of things might you do and feel that you don't think you could do and feel today?

2

Give Up Resentment; Get Back Love

(1) What Is Resentment?

Our natural ability to remember offenses

It's said that elephants have the best memories of any animal. For the sake of pachyderms everywhere, I hope that's not true. Because if elephants have memories anywhere near as good as humans, then one thing's for sure: there's an awfully large number of angry elephants running around the golden fields of Africa.

The average guy won't remember what he had for lunch yesterday. He doesn't know where he took his wife on their sixth date. He can't recall the last name of that college history professor he liked so much.

But if somebody once insulted him? If somebody actually did him wrong? Why, suddenly that same guy, who can't conjure 95 (or 99?) percent of the things that ever happened in his whole life, displays a memory that would shame an elephant capable of recalling where he'd hid a single peanut fourteen years ago.

43

When it comes to harboring resentments, we're veritable masters. Doesn't matter what kind of person we're talking about, either. Highly educated folks with lots of advanced degrees, people who never went to high school, others who've traveled the globe, those who've never been anywhere but their village—with rare exception, every person in the world nurses their resentments as if they were the most precious things in the world.

And there are some good reasons we do this, too. That we harbor resentments as we do isn't all bad. Much of it, for instance, is born of the simple fact that in life we all have many important lessons to learn. Like the child who learns the hard way not to put his hand on a hot burner, so we, as we grow, must learn and remember what it looks and feels like to get burned.

It's by way of people doing us wrong that we learn to detect the kinds of signals we all need to be at least somewhat adept at reading if, in the future, we want to protect ourselves from continually getting hurt in that same way. We might call those early slights and resentments "vaccinations" against future maladies that would be much more painful.

But just like a glass of red wine can be good for you, and several bottles in an evening isn't, learning from the times you've been slighted is good for you, while harboring resentment isn't. And just as with drinking too much, harboring resentments wrecks your perceptions, distorts your emotions, and ultimately turns you into someone other people, if given a choice, will avoid.

Tending to the garden of your resentments

As I was thinking about what resentments mean to the person who too tightly holds on to them, an image popped into my head of a flower garden with weeds growing in it. I then remembered a friend named John, who once told me about how, as a kid, part of his chores every weekend was to clear his family's backyard of weeds. I phoned John and asked him to retell that story.

44

"Well, Steve," he said,

I can tell you that I didn't much like weeding. It was dirty work, and hard: some of those weeds were like little trees out there, with long, tough roots that knew a thing or two about clinging to mother earth. You really had to dig those things out.

Now, I'm not saying the only reason I thought this was because I really, really didn't want to have to keep picking weeds every Saturday, while my friends were all off in the park near my house playing ball and having all kinds of fun I *knew* I should have been having with them. But the truth is it began to occur to me while I was out there shredding my fingers trying to wrestle from the ground yet another dandelion with roots that seemed to go all the way to China, that it was awfully random of someone, somewhere, to decide that weeds were *weeds,* and therefore undesirable, while all the other plants around the weeds *weren't* weeds, and so were desirable.

It seemed so random. I didn't see any big difference. They were both green. They both wanted to live. Sure, they were small and pretty scraggly—but the dandelion sprouted flowers! Why were *those* considered any worse than the other flowers we had growing out there? Why should one kind of flower or plant be considered *lower* than other kinds? They were all just plants, man!

(Remember, Steve—this was in the late sixties and early seventies. Down with the man, man! Flower power!)

So, thinking I was really on to something, I decided to one day pull the plants and leave the weeds. I knew that if I explained to my father ahead of time what I wanted to do, he'd argue against it and stop me. But if I showed him, he would definitely get it and praise me for opening his eyes to the injustice of the plant system we'd been so blindly following for so long.

I pulled all the plants out of this big section of our backyard, and I left the weeds.

Guess what? My dad, in spectacular fashion, failed to appreciate my enlightening experiment with a non-prejudicial approach to plants. And unlike the plants I'd pulled, I was very definitely grounded.

Isn't that exactly how we treat our resentments sometimes? Whether or not we've realized it, we've been nurturing predatory weeds at the expense of caring for beautiful flowers.

John was just a boy when he failed to appreciate the damage weeds do, the harm they cause to lovely plants, the way they suck the life out of everything else around them.

If you're cherishing invasive resentments at the cost of what really should be flourishing in your life's garden, what's your excuse?

There's no such thing as a resentmentplace

I love a fireplace. There's just nothing better on a cold, wintery night than a roaring fire. Heck, I like fires so much it doesn't even have to be very cool outside for me to enjoy one.

When I lived in sunny Southern California, where people practically convolute cold weather with the dawn of the apocalypse, I didn't *need* a fire any more often than I needed snow tires. But did that stop me? No way. My wife only had to say, "Bit chilly in here, isn't it?" and before she could reach for a sweater, I'd have whipped up a blaze so roaring you'd think we were cabin-bound in the Arctic.

Of all things about a fireplace, though, do you know what I like best? It's not the wonderful feeling I get when I'm inside next to all that pleasant warmth. It's not the way a crackling fire on a cold night invites my wife and me to cuddle in front of it. It's not how the family gathers around it to talk and sing and share the kind of precious times that make being a husband and father so rewarding.

It's not even that they allow me to build and start fires, which I love to do. (I flatter myself that the most resourceful Eagle Scout can't beat my technique for sculpting a fire-ready mound so perfect I feel it's almost a shame to put a match to it.)

No. *My favorite thing about a fireplace is the way it keeps fire from burning down the house.* It contains. The fire never leaves.

Inside a home, fire has its . . . well, place. That's the way it should be.

Unfortunately, when it comes to resentment, there's no place in us that holds it. Our inner homes don't come with a "resentmentplace." If we stoke the fires of our resentment, they escape whatever little soul compartment they may have started in, and they begin spreading everywhere within us.

Resentment can't be enclosed. It doesn't sit and stay. It becomes within us a virus, taking on a life of its own, increasingly invading everything we feel, think, say, and do.

What's the answer? *We must learn to pour water on the fires of our resentment.* If we don't—if instead we poke at it, toss on more kindling, and tend to it like we would a regular fire—then watch out. We'll be continuing on a path absolutely covered with and surrounded by dry leaves and needles and other highly flammable stuff just waiting and ready to burn.

Down that way lies hell.

(2) What Resentment Does to Your Life

Makes your past dominate your present

Have you ever known somebody so stuck in their past she couldn't move into her future? We all probably have, at least once—someone who spends so much time looking backward that she can't seem to ever see the road ahead.

Robert was one such man. He was a good guy; I knew him when he was in college. It was there that he met the woman of his dreams.

"Steve!" he (almost literally) cried to me one day. "I met her!"

"Who?"

"Her! *Her!* The one!"

"The one?"

"The one! The one for me! The one God himself put on this earth just for me to love!"

"*Oh!*" I said. "The *one*. *That* one. Congratulations! Who is she?"

So Bob, breathlessly, told me all about the wonderful, dazzling, exciting girl he'd met.

It was fantastic to see him so obviously taken. "Taken" isn't the word for it, either. He was *gone*. He wasn't even around. My usually rational, calm, collected, intellectually disciplined friend had turned into a giggling puddle of sheer adoration.

"Holy cow!" I said when he was finished. (Or, to put it more exactly, when I finally had to interrupt him; it was getting late.) "It does sound like she's the one."

"She is." He fell back in his seat, as if merely *considering* the perfection of Rebecca had thoroughly exhausted him. "She's very definitely the one."

Happily, Rebecca felt the same way about Bob. Watching them together—as cute and affirming a thing as you could ever want to see—would have turned the original Ebenezer Scrooge into a gushing schoolboy.

"You did it," I'd say to Bob. "You found her. Hallelujah, brother."

After they'd been inseparable for about a year, they announced their engagement.

After another year, a beaming Bob waited at the altar for his beautiful bride to make her grand, breathtaking entrance.

He waited.

And he waited.

And waited.

We all waited.

Rebecca never showed.

Turns out, she was in Mexico. She'd run off with an old boyfriend.

What a gift, *not* to be stuck with someone who'd leave you standing there alone rather than call, sit down together, and talk it all through.

However, Bob didn't see it that way, and it broke his heart.

How would you respond to that kind of heartbreak?

Bob never married. He hasn't yet, anyway—and he waited at that altar a long time ago. He's too bitter about what happened in his past to live in his present and move on to his future. The resentment he feels toward Rebecca is not the enflamed, seething miasma it became after the sheer, raw pain of his initial hurt wore off. However, the bottom line is, Rebecca wounded him so deeply that he no longer trusts love.

Resentment from what could be behind him has been allowed to ruin what's still before him.

I recently sent Bob two verses. The first was 1 Peter 5:10:

In his kindness God called you to share in his eternal glory by means of Christ Jesus. So after you have suffered a little while, he will restore, support, and strengthen you, and he will place you on a firm foundation.

The other was Romans 3:10:

As the Scriptures say,

"No one is righteous—
not even one."

I pray that Bob lets the power of these words fully sink into his heart. If you're harboring a deep resentment from a past injury, I deeply hope that you do the same.

Taints how you see the future

We've just considered the tragic case of a man whose heart was so pierced by a woman that ultimately *he's* done himself more harm by nurturing his resentment than *she* did harm in the first place. Rebecca could only hurt Bob so much; the rest he has allowed his resentment to do to him.

Bob's situation, though, isn't common—at least, I hope it's not. The resentment he's cherished has dominated his life. Usually what happens with people is that resentment *taints* their life rather than out-and-out rules it.

And unlike with Bob, the pain that gives birth to the resentment most typically interfering with a person living God's best for him frequently isn't traceable to a single event. It's not usually this simple (insofar as you'd ever want to call such suffering "simple").

I wish the resentment most people harbor *were* so directly attributable. I wish I could talk with someone about what had caused her hurt and led to her resentment—to find out that *one day* she was wounded, that *one time* someone victimized her, that the resentment choking the quality out of her life and blocking her experience of the richness God has waiting for her has been caused by *one thing*.

"Well, there's your obstacle!" I could say. "Let's talk about that terrible event. Let's talk about what he did to you. Let's talk about how it hurt you, and what the pain from it has done to your life. Let's pray together that Jesus restores you from the damage this engendered in you. And let's pray that the person who did this is delivered of the pain he surely is carrying, the pain he allowed to drive him into hurting another person—*you*—probably in something close to the way someone once hurt him." And then we could begin focusing on bringing healing to her from that wrong.

Oh, I wish. That would be as if the lights throughout a mansion seemed haywire—blinking on and off, sometimes working, sometimes not—and I, the electrician, went inside, found the fusebox, and located an unscrewed fuse.

"*Here's* what's gone wrong," I'd say. Then I'd just give it a few twists and, presto. Every room in that whole place would light right up. Finished!

If *only* it were that simple. Of course, it's not. Usually, the causes for the resentments people lug around are buried deep in the past, and most often they consist of myriad, complicated little components.

And usually, the resentments don't paralyze; rather, they tend to "disable" or "partially cripple." It's not so much that people clinging to resentment can't see anything; it's that they're slightly blinded, all the time. Their well isn't poisoned; instead, it's tainted.

But that taint, whatever its concentration, is a permeating enemy. The pervasive infiltration of resentment prevents those with infected wells from being refreshed, nourished, and vital. From being healthy. From truly living.

You're always expecting the worst

Once more, it's not so much that old resentments tend to ruin you as that they tend to compromise your life in a way and to a degree that, ultimately, you're going to have to deal with and get over if you're ever going to step out of what you're accustomed to and instead start experiencing God's best.

Know *how* resentments from the past most often compromise a person's life? By ruining the way he sees the future. In that respect, what happened to Bob at the altar *is* typical, insofar as it made him want to never again commit himself to love. He felt that if he ever did, the worst surely would happen. He'd be abandoned again. His heart would be broken again.

"No thanks," said Bob. "I'll pass." And so Bob, in very key ways, said no to his future.

We all do this, to some extent—to an extent I'd like us to all get rid of. We look ahead with vision tainted by what's behind. If we've been badly disappointed or hurt before, we can't help but assume, to one degree or another, that *that* will happen again. So—usually without even being aware of why we're doing it—we begin to guard ourselves against anything that even smells like whatever once engendered the kinds of pain that in turn led to our lasting resentments.

I have a friend who has a real heart for dogs. He understands dogs so well and is so patient and loving with them that he has taken to adopting ones that have been abused.

51

"It's just the saddest thing," he said the other day. "But a dog that's been beat in the past can sometimes get very mean. Sometimes a dog like that is so sure it's going to get beaten again that it wants to attack just about anything that moves. It's only got enemies. And a dog like that will very often have a particular kind of person or even thing that will trigger its reactive response.

"Part of what I have to do with a dog that's clearly on the defensive from something in its past is find out, as much as I can, what kinds of triggers it associates with the pain it once suffered. One thing I do is lead him around my garage. Sometimes he'll see a broom, say, and just start barking and jumping around. Then I'll know: somebody used to hit him with a broom."

We're the same way. If we got hit in some awful way before, we expect to get hit that way again.

That's the pattern we need to break. The future, for us, isn't about abuse and resentment. It's about the love of Jesus. And that never hurts.

(3) How to Give Up Resentment

Look hard at who and what you "resent"

I have a friend who used to carry around a crippling resentment, one of which he wasn't aware. The person he "resented" was his own mother, and I qualify this with quotation marks because here I don't mean "resentment" in the way it's most typically used and understood.

If someone purposefully hurts you, it's easy to resent her. It's easy to be clear on why you resent her, too: she hurt you; you resent her for hurting you. Not a terribly complex emotional trajectory. Pretty straightforward.

But what if you resent somebody for something she couldn't help but do? That's not just a tad more but a *lot* more complicated. Plus, what if that person is—as with my friend—your mom? What if, a long time ago, she (or your dad) hurt you in a way that wasn't her (or his) fault?

Well, then you've got a real psychological problem. Then you'll probably need a counselor like me (or maybe one better than me). That's a tough knot to untie all by yourself.

My friend's mother died of cancer when he was just a boy. And even though he of course loved her, and even though she couldn't do anything to stop the disease that took only eight months (post-discovery) to kill her, he found himself as an adult always expecting the worst to happen in his life.

He was a guy who apparently had a dark cloud constantly hovering overhead. He always tainted what he said with a little negativity. Nothing was ever quite good enough or right enough. No one was ever sufficiently capable.

It wasn't that he actively complained; it was much more subtle. He consistently, perpetually made it clear, in some way, that, at best, he anticipated the worst. To put it bluntly, his life reflected the truth that he didn't expect much out of it.

As it turned out, most of the negativity he was carrying around stemmed from deep-down resentment toward his mother for dying—essentially, for abandoning him. It took him a long time to figure out finally that he did carry it, and feel it, and that it was holding him back from experiencing God's best.

He did what we all must do: look long and hard to discover the causes. We must ask Jesus to help us find and root out that which, without him, might always keep us handicapped.

Put blame where it belongs

When we harbor resentments, we're making a very wrong choice. We're taking stuff, bad stuff—stuff that rightfully belongs to someone else—and making it our own. This doesn't make any sense.

Imagine (because this really did not happen) that one day I'm home working when I happen to look out my window. There I see my theoretical neighbor from down the street, "Mr. Goaway," stroll up, step onto my front porch, drop a big, ratty, held-together-by-duct-tape suitcase, then leave.

"Wait! Mr. Goaway! Hey!" I call. He doesn't hear me; I hadn't wanted to scream too loudly, because my wife and kids are taking a nap. And it's when they're all quietly asleep that I get some of my best office work done.

But I digress.

So I go out to my porch, and there's the bag. Assuming that despite the appearance this must be something important, I drag the surprisingly heavy load inside. I close the door behind me—and that's when I notice a distinct emanation. The odor is pretty bad, like cigarettes and body odor.

"Misty won't like this," I say. And I'm right. She can't stand cigarette smoke *and* prefers that I wear deodorant. "Oh well—might as well bring it into the living room."

I clear a place on the coffee table and set down the bag. I pop open its rusted, cracked clasps and lift its top. Mr. Goaway's suitcase is . . . stuffed full of moldy food and Marlboro butts? And is that an old *sock* in there?

"What's that, honey?" says my wife. She's up!

"Something Mr. Goaway just left on our porch."

"What's that smell?" She comes over, looks in, and screams. She wants that *thing* out of the house. *Now.*

Guess what I do, though? I don't take it out. I leave it inside. Not only that, I leave it right there on the table. I insist that this foul haul of garbage become an everyday feature; I want it integrated with our lives.

Wouldn't that be a destructively absurd thing for me to do?

Yet that's exactly what we do when we embrace, as our own, resentments caused by what other people have brought into our lives.

Don't be like me with Goaway's suitcase. It's *his*. Just as I shouldn't have welcomed it into my home and thus made it my own, so you shouldn't accept into your heart resentments caused by something someone else decided to unload.

Look at your resentments; find out what led to them; then send all that nasty, stinking stuff packing to where it belongs.

The futility of wanting to change what you can't

Most of us are at least somewhat familiar with the opening lines of the initially untitled, now-famous Serenity Prayer, attributed to Reinhold Neibuhr:

> God, grant me the serenity
> > To accept the things I cannot change;
> > Courage to change the things I can;
> > And wisdom to know the difference.

It's an excellent prayer to apply to a whole lot of life-dynamics; in fact, I can't think of any sort of internal struggle a person might endure in which it wouldn't be helpful to remember. There's certainly no mystery as to why it was adapted by, and has played such an important role in, Alcoholics Anonymous and every other twelve-step program meeting today.

What makes the Serenity Prayer so powerful is the way it directly points to one of the most important life-truths we so often get so very, very wrong. In a way—and certainly when it comes to our relationship with God—that thing we get wrong is always the *same thing* we get wrong.

We become prideful.

We become sure we can handle everything. Sure we can change things. Sure we can cure it all.

We become certain that, when all is said and done, the buck stops with us. Certain that a whole bunch of stuff completely out of our control actually is in our control—and, more so, actually is our responsibility.

This is what happens with most of us, in terms of handling resentment. We mistakenly think that *we'll* fix whatever led to it—that we can bring the other guy to understand the error of his ways and take responsibility for what he did, or even (and this is always the hook for me) that we can change him. We're prone to believing that since what he did or said to us was *wrong*, we can show him the wrongness, and once he's realized it (thanks to us, of course), he'll repent of his harmful ways and make everything right. All will be well with us. Peace and harmony will everywhere prevail.

Occasionally, something like that happens. Most of the time, it doesn't. People usually are too defensive, too invested in seeming justified in what they say and do; "getting them" to apologize for or even acknowledge the error of something they've done or said can be like separating a bone from a Rottweiler. Even if you're able to do it, neither the process nor the result will be pretty.

When it comes to people who've given you reason to feel resentment, consider what, if anything, about the results of their actions or words that you can, and can't, change.

Do try to change what you can. But forget and let go of the rest. As an old Mother Goose poem has it:

> For every ailment under the sun
> There is a remedy, or there is none.
> If there be one, try to find it;
> If there be none, never mind it.

(4) Gaining Back Love

Remembering that God is love

After you begin the journey toward being free of resentments that block you from living out God's best, at some point along the way you're going to run into a wall. The wall will be standing between you and your destination.

And there you'll be, still weighed down under your heavy baggage, unable to move forward.

As you stand there, hunched over, looking up at that high, thick barrier, what you'll realize is that you've reached the "end of the road." You'll have gone as far as you can.

When it comes to your resentments, you'll find you can't let go. *Can't* forgive. *Can't* forget. That suitcase just isn't something you can drop at will. Your grip on it, you'll discover, is stronger than you are.

Your resentments won't at all feel like they're something separate from you. That luggage set you've been hauling around is more like part of your arm than anything you can just toss to the side of the road and reject.

Presently, it's your burden. However it got there, *currently,* it's yours.

What's it costing you to continue dragging resentment around? *Love.*

Again, resentment blinds you. It ties you in knots. It bogs you down. It holds you back so you can't move forward.

You can't love when you can't see, can't feel, can't experience, can't grow.

So what to do when you've hit that wall?

As a Christian, what should you always do when you've come up against a challenge you don't feel up to? *Turn to God.*

And while that's always the very best thing you can do, when it comes to unburdening yourself from resentment it's absolutely essential.

Your resentments are keeping you from love.

And what's God?

Anyone who does not love does not know God, for God is love.

—1 John 4:8

There it is. Even if you didn't have John's plain and simple language assuring you that God *is* love, you'd know it. You know the truth of it in your heart. You know that sharing his love—in proving its unimaginable vastness through the sacrifice of his son, Jesus Christ—is what God's all about.

You know that God has the strong, steady love you need. And you know that when it comes to walls or *any* obstacles, nothing can stop or even hinder God; nothing can defeat what's all-powerful and all-conquering. That's love.

So turn to him. Ask him for his love.

Then step back. The wall that's blocking your way will start tumbling down.

Allowing yourself to shed your resentment

I like to run. I'm not too bad at it, either—not as good as I used to be, maybe, but I still get out there and do it.

I love the way running makes me feel. And just like with most things I care about, when it comes to running I find it helpful to establish goals. So I'll determine, for example, to run a certain number of miles a week, and then I'll do my best to meet the mark.

Sometimes I'll set a target I know is pretty far out there. I like a challenge, though, and if I don't set goals for myself, who will? Maybe I'll hear about an upcoming public race in or near my neighborhood; I'll set a goal of competing in it. (Notice I said *competing*, not winning. I like to run and can't deny, generally speaking, that I like to win, but I'm not so delusional about my ability that I really ever expect those two things to join up.)

Over the years, I've noticed something: no matter how far I know I'm going to run, the last stretch is nearly impossible.

Not long ago I ran a 5K. I know that distance; I've run it many times. Before the race I ran it quite often, training for it. When the day came, I knew perfectly well I was capable. No problem, right?

And yet, in the final stretch, the same thing happened that always happens right when I'm closing in on the end. I felt I could barely make it. I was ready; I was fit; I knew the distance . . . and still, during the last half mile or so, I felt like I'd run twenty miles instead of just over three.

There's something about knowing you're close to finishing that suddenly increases the sense of difficulty. Not every time, of course, or about everything, but overall, this often happens.

If it happens to you as you move from clinging to resentment toward letting it go, here's some advice: give yourself permission. *Allow* yourself to let go of this thing that for a long time has been integral to your identity.

Frequently, in a crucial stretch of seizing the life God most wants you to have, what's necessary at the end of shedding resentment is simply, clearly, and resolutely telling yourself that you deserve to be free of it.

Because you do. What Jesus has done for you means that toxins like resentment have no right to taint you. In the end, it's that basic.

Even so, if you get stuck in the process of saying good-bye to your resentments, be sure you get whatever help is needed to let them go entirely.

Opening yourself up to the constancy of God's love

Our culture essentially encourages us to see everything as being in flux. That "things change," or that reality doesn't have any truly consistent, reliable characteristic, is a commonly accepted perception of the world in which we live. Does *anything* ever really stay the same? Well, *things* don't.

I bought a yellow convertible when I turned forty. I still have it; I think it's beautiful. There was one thing I knew was true at the time: it would remain beautiful only if I kept it detailed. So I've faithfully washed it, and I've waxed it until my arms fell off (or at least until my arms fell asleep while I've been waiting for the people I was pay-ing to finish waxing . . .).

My lovely car is a bit weathered now, but people still drive up beside me and give a thumbs-up.

I wrecked it a couple times, but it was repaired perfectly.

I left it out in the rain with its top down, but it dried.

And I *have* driven it, a lot. I've thoroughly enjoyed spending time in it.

Nevertheless, time, being time, inevitably took its toll.

Of course it did. That's what time does. It changes things—everything.

Nothing in our world is constant. A thing is always transforming from what it was to what it is to what it will become.

If I'd worshiped that convertible so much that perfection in it was "the constant standard," I'd be one heartbroken man. Instead, its natural weathering has drawn me to enjoying what it is. It has character and charm because of change; I let go, long ago, of false hope about my car always staying perfectly the same.

That's *this* world, where everything changes. But in God's world? *There* is something that never does. That something is God. God is permanent. God is eternal. God, always and forever, is God.

And what's the very essence of God's nature? Love. We serve a God of love. God showed us how deeply and how constantly he loves us by sending his only son, Jesus, who gave himself—gave his whole life—for us.

Open yourself up to that truth. Let yourself know that God's love for you is unwavering. Trade in your old resentments, and the old you that nurtured them, for a new you with a new life in Christ. And read Psalm 36:5–9, a passage absolutely saturated with God's love for us:

> Your unfailing love, O Lord, is as vast as the heavens;
>   your faithfulness reaches beyond the clouds.

Your righteousness is like the mighty mountains,
your justice like the ocean depths.
You care for people and animals alike, O Lord.
How precious is your unfailing love, O God!
All humanity finds shelter
in the shadow of your wings.
You feed them from the abundance of your own house,
letting them drink from your river of delights.
For you are the fountain of life,
the light by which we see.

(5) Living a Life Filled With Love

Enjoying God's love for yourself

The truth is, most of us *aren't* very prone to being selfish. Now, I know that sounds untrue. But hear me out, please.

We *feel* selfish, don't we? I know I do.

I'm always ready to have better things and to get the stuff I want. Yes, I like the idea of self-sacrifice, and I can be reasonably good at delaying what I want immediately for something better to come, or at putting others ahead of myself. (Or, at least I've actually done that a couple of times.) Still, if I'm honest with myself, I must admit that as hard as I try to always put others first, usually, in one way or another, I manage to place my own needs at the front of the line. I'd like not to be this way, yet I am. No question, most people are.

It's fairly obvious, then, that we tend to be pretty selfish when it comes to "things of this world": money or precious objects or flattery or power (real or perceived) or the attention of others. In that sense, most of us have a more than robust selfish streak. But where we tend to be the opposite of selfish is the one place we *should* be *most* selfish: *taking for ourselves God's love.*

There we tend to be hesitant. We often don't allow ourselves to feel the sheer joy of what it is to be loved by God. Because that's what it is to be loved by God: joy. What could be more joyous to the human spirit than knowing—not wondering, not hoping, not guessing, but *knowing*—that God loves you? What greater delight could anyone ever want? It's the biggest prize. *Nothing* compares to the God of love. Nothing is more guaranteed to bring happiness.

Instead of enjoying God's constant and abiding love for us, though, what do many of us do? Get reticent. Shy away. Wonder whether we're "worthy" of the love God already has assured us is ours for the asking!

Don't do that to yourself. A crucial part of shedding your resentments is trading that negative, useless energy for the beaming, fresh, invigorating love of God himself. *Revel in that love.* Call it what it is: yours.

It's yours. All of it belongs to you.

Don't be shy about that. Be as greedy for God's love as you possibly can be, because God wants you to have it all.

This is the one kind of selfishness you can really, really enjoy. Don't deny yourself that pleasure.

Sharing God's love with others

People say it's always better to give than to receive. I like the idea of that being true. And in fact, it is. We all know how good it is to give something to another person. Part of the real delight of birthdays and all kinds of celebrations is how enjoyable it is to give someone a gift we know (or hope!) is perfect for them. We love to see a big smile come over their face as they open the gift, as they take into their own hands tangible evidence of our personal care; we selected, bought, wrapped, and presented them with something clearly meant as a symbol of our love.

Fun as it is to give gifts, I'd be the last to pretend it's not also pretty great getting them. I love receiving a present. Sometimes I don't even want to open a gift, because I don't want the part where

I just received it to end. It's the anticipation that, for me, is almost as good as getting whatever it actually is.

If gifts are wonderful to give and wonderful to get, how much more wonderful is it to get and give the greatest gift of all: God's love. And unlike with a normal gift, when you give God's love, you get *more* of it!

Think about this for a moment. With what other kind of present do you receive more once you've handed it over? Talk about a miracle!

Imagine handing someone a fifty, then looking into your wallet to see a new hundred-dollar bill in its place. How happy would that make you? And wouldn't you then give that hundred away, just to see if it would happen again? And when it did—when you discovered that, astonishingly, two hundreds had replaced your one—wouldn't you start running around, handing out as much cash to as many people as possible?

You bet you would.

Well, *do it*. There's nothing more valuable than the love of God.

As you increasingly become free of the things, like resentment, that have kept love out of you, you'll realize that now love is welling up within you. Take it and hand it out. See how much more love keeps on taking its place.

Go! Give! Share with others!

It's the best investment you will ever make.

Putting God's love into action

Earlier I wrote about the convertible I love. One thing I like best about it is how much it *looks* like it wants to be driven. It just has the look of a car that wants to be out on the road, going fast.

That's exactly what it does like doing, too. I don't know if I'd go so far as some of my more fanatical auto-loving buddies would, to say that my car has a soul, but it definitely seems to have one very strong desire: to be driven.

63

Looking at that car, you wouldn't think of doing anything else with it. Not "Gee, what a nice planter box," or "Gosh, that is the most aesthetically pleasing shopping cart I've seen."

No. One look at that machine, and all you'll think is, "Who has the keys to this thing? Let's *drive* it!" (It's a 1971, so do be a bit careful. We recently sang "Happy Fortieth Birthday" to my old yellow car.)

That's what I always thought when I saw it. Then I'd remember: *I have the keys—it's mine!* And then, of course, I'd realize I'd lost them; for a man with ADHD, car keys are little living creatures that scurry away to hide in impossible places at the slightest possible provocation.

But even if yet again I was keyless and clueless, that car *was* made to drive. Engine, tires, trunk, wheel, chassis . . . other parts I could name if I knew a lot more about cars . . . all of it was made for one reason and purpose.

We're like cars. And not just because we, too, have gas. We're like cars because, just like they're designed to be driven, we're designed to put God's love into action.

That's what we're for. That's why God made us. We're not intended to sit around, feeling God's love, then doing nothing about what that love makes us experience. A person who says he's filled with God's love but never does anything that helps others is full of something, indeed, but it isn't God's love.

The resentments you've been carrying around are all about you. They're about something wrong done to you, about emotions you feel (or have felt). Resentment is all energy concerned with, and wrapped up in, you.

When you lose them, and replace them with the liberating glory of God's love, it finally becomes not about you. That's when, free to love people the way God loves you, living becomes about doing exactly that: loving others.

That's when you find the key to your whole life. That's when you start driving.

Questions for Discussion

1. What do you think, right now, is the strongest resentment you're carrying around inside?

2. What do you think your resentments cost you? Do they really compromise the quality of your life? Are they so natural or "normal" to you that you're not really aware of them?

3. If a person has deep-seated resentments against one or both parents, do you think it's truly possible to shed them? Do you think he can, in that realm, rewrite the script of his past, of where it's brought him today?

4. Do you think any of the resentments you carry affect how you see the future? Do you have any attitudes about people or events that might have as much to do with your resentments as with the objective facts?

5. What's the most recent thing you did whereby you shared God's love with another person?

3

Give Up Fear; Get Back Trust

(1) What Is Fear?

Everyday worries

Fear is one of those words that, like *love*, can have such a broad range of meaning that it's hard to nail down the exact expression you're aiming for. I think we all understand the biggest fears in life: fear of dying, say, or fear of losing a loved one—strong, natural fears to which we're all susceptible.

Most of life, though, doesn't really or directly involve such huge fears. Yes, there are times when large-scale and even overwhelming fears come into play, but usually, in daily living, these are not the ones that block us from trust. They do block us from "big trust"—that is to say, they bump us up against our most powerful and most complete fear, that God isn't taking care of everything and that everything ultimately isn't going to be okay. However, normally our ability to trust isn't so obviously compromised. Standardly, and subtly, such that we barely notice them eating away at the trust we need in order to live God's best, it's the small fears that are getting to us.

Take, for instance, dry cleaning. The reason I thought of this: just today I took some clothes to my neighborhood dry cleaner. I like this business; they do good work. In fact, my stuff always comes back *seemingly* having been owned by someone who knows how to eat without spilling. (I frequently end up with a messy condition I call "snacker's shirt.")

Well, my dry cleaner was sold recently, and so today I didn't see the former owner, who used to run the place, standing behind the counter. Now there was a new person, a young woman, entirely polite and apparently good-natured. All the same, as I left the establishment, I couldn't help but feel fear that the new operators wouldn't handle my things like the old owners had.

Silly, right? For one thing, I doubt they decided to overhaul the cleaning process entirely: when you buy something, usually you do it because you like the way it already works. For another, that the new person was young certainly doesn't mean she's incapable of managing her responsibility. Further, the people who pick up and process the bags of clothing—and the ones who actually do the cleaning—maybe or probably haven't changed at all.

"Fear for the well-being of my clothes" is a small one. With every day of our lives come a thousand such fears. But we need to take note of them because, in a very real way, they're all microversions of the one biggest fear: that God isn't in control.

God *is* in control. It *is* going to be all right. I can relax about my stuff—even if it does get ruined, so what? Maybe that will be God's way of telling me he'd like to see me in sweats and T-shirts more often. And if that's what God wants, then that's exactly how I'll dress.

Hey, now I hope they ruin my clothes!

Big-picture fears

Messengers arrived from the home of Jairus, the leader of the synagogue. They told him, "Your daughter is dead. There's no use troubling the Teacher now."

But Jesus overheard them and said to Jairus, "Don't be afraid. Just have faith."

Then Jesus stopped the crowd and wouldn't let anyone go with him except Peter, James, and John (the brother of James). When they came to the home of the synagogue leader, Jesus saw much commotion and weeping and wailing. He went inside and asked, "Why all this commotion and weeping? The child isn't dead; she's only asleep."

The crowd laughed at him. But he made them all leave, and he took the girl's father and mother and his three disciples into the room where the girl was lying. Holding her hand, he said to her, "*Talitha koum*," which means "Little girl, get up!" And the girl, who was twelve years old, immediately stood up and walked around! They were overwhelmed and totally amazed.

—Mark 5:35–42

This, one of my favorite Bible stories, marvelously demonstrates that, if we're to live with the wondrous trust that comes from knowing we're protected by a benevolent God who will never fail us, we must learn how to give up our "big fears." In this case, the fear of death.

If we trust in God, our fears will be shown to be nothing. That's what this account deftly teaches us.

"*Don't be afraid. Just have faith.*" That's Jesus telling us, in the plainest, simplest terms, all we need to know. We should never let fear block out our faith in God. He said it; therefore, I believe it.

The girl . . . immediately stood up and walked around! What more do we need to know about the power of Jesus and the glory that awaits us if we'll only put our faith in him? Here, in one sentence, is everything we could possibly need in order to never again let any fear, no matter its perceived size or strength, stand in the way of our faith in God.

In the same vein, two revelations in this statement can keep us immersed in joy every day of our lives.

First, Christ has the power. Who but God himself can raise the dead? It's the greatest miracle of all; *Jesus is exactly who he says he is.*

Second, don't miss the "one big truth" that, if we truly and completely believed, would eliminate all our fears forever: *no one who places faith in Jesus Christ ever faces death alone.*

Underlying fear that you just don't measure up

What God wants most is for us to give back to him all of ourselves. He wants our ideas, our minds, our hearts, our ambitions, our desires—he wants everything. And most of us Jesus followers do a decent job of giving him our all, of surrendering everything we have to give. We know God wants us to give him our all; we at least strive to give it to him.

But usually, at some point along the way toward making our "all" God's property and purview, we stop. We bring *almost* all of ourselves to him yet find that when it comes to some last, final little "bit," we balk. We hesitate. We hold back.

We tell God to stop. We tell *God*—and consider the impertinence of this—that he has enough!

What is it we most often tend to hold in reserve? What's inside that we not only think God can't see but also don't want him to see? That we don't want to share with him? That we want to keep to ourselves?

Nine out of ten times? It's *the conviction that, ultimately, we really, truly, simply aren't good enough.* This lies at the core of so much that keeps us rooted in fear and thus held short of enjoying God's very best for us: our innate suspicion that we're unworthy of the love of our Creator and Sustainer. That God's "full love" is one we don't deserve. That the best of it is reserved, really, for those who, through the way they live and the purity of their acts and thoughts, merit *him* in a way we can't, and won't, ever.

When it comes to once and for all handing over to God utterly everything we have to give, we don't. We keep "that part" to ourselves.

Thus we show that, in the end, we'd rather hang on to fear than trust in God.

No good. That just won't do!

What must we know and believe in order to allow ourselves, finally, to bring all of ourselves to God—even that part of us we're sure he'll reject?

Not much. We don't have to know much to realize that we'll experience more of God's love when we're broken and weak.

Everyone, deep down, even if it's concealed under countless layers of self-protection, thinks he or she isn't really good enough.

But God doesn't expect our perfection—in fact, he's the only way we can move toward healing and growth in the first place. He wants us to acknowledge our brokenness, then bring it to him.

He wants us to trust him. He wants us to entrust all of ourselves to him—even those "parts" that, mistakenly, we think he doesn't already know about.

(2) What Fear Does to Your Life

Futilely trying to keep things frozen in time

I once knew a woman who tried to freeze time. She lived in a big place with nothing but cats. Not one or two, either. Or four. Or eight. She had . . . well, I don't know *how* many.

Her huge, two-story house had at least ten rooms, and it seemed to me every doorway led to at least ten cats, lounging about as if they'd died and gone to kitty heaven. Which, for all I know, they had—it's hard to imagine any cat anywhere having a better life than those fortunate felines who lived with Mrs. P. (I hope you aren't thinking I chose that initial for her last name not because it actually started with "P" but because her whole place smelled like cat pee. If you *are* thinking that, then let me just say I'm appalled you'd think me capable of stooping to anything so sophomoric. Appalled!)

When I met her, Mrs. P. had been a widow for about twenty years. She was living in the same home she'd shared a very long time with her husband. She was a devout Christian, one of those women I personally tend to like, insofar as she had a regular daily routine of radio programs she never failed to miss. She'd keep an eye on the morning clock, and when eleven rolled around she'd stop everything she was doing (usually one thing or another with her cats), make herself tea, put coffee cake on a plate, sit in her easy chair, and turn on the radio she kept on a table right beside it.

In life, though, she was failing. Her home was run down; she never cleaned; she barely went outside; as much as I do like them, that many cats in one house isn't healthy, and they qualified her as an official pet hoarder.

As I got to know Mrs. P. better, I came to realize that fear was holding her back. Her husband had always been the one who took care of business, went out in the world and made the money, fixed the house, tended to the yard. When he died, she tried to freeze her life right where it was.

Nearly a quarter of a century later, that clearly wasn't working.

It never works. We can no sooner stop time than we can stop ocean waves from breaking on the shore.

Sincere Christian though Mrs. P. was, she was showing, through her (benign, certainly) efforts to halt the sun in its place, that she wasn't really trusting God. She was, at heart, living fearfully.

Don't you do that. Let life move forward; *participate* in the grand design of God's ongoing creation.

Trust him!

Cutting off relationships before they can grow

One of the indicators in a person's life that he's clinging to fear and thereby allowing it to keep him from experiencing God's best is that, while he seems to have many friends and some intimate relationships, he doesn't truly have either. They aren't *really* friends; his relationships aren't *truly* intimate.

Have you ever known a person who seems to have a million friends and acquaintances but, when you get to know her better, you realize that, all appearances to the contrary, she actually invests in and maintains few if any intimate connections? A person who seems to be at the hub of a vast array of parties and events and other happenings—and yet who, once you're more familiar with the true nature of her relationships, turns out to be, deep down, an exceedingly lonely person?

It's the strangest thing. Often it's the very people most adept at bringing others into their lives who, in the end, are the least able or willing to sustain long-term, intimate bonds.

I get fooled by this all the time. I'll meet someone who seems genuine; he's so warm, so open, and so willing that, before long, I'll count him as a friend. I begin to give of myself to him. I make my resources available to him. I take the time to check in—to visit, to call, to make sure that if he needs anything, I find a way to help provide it.

I do my best to be a friend.

I'm guessing you already know what happens: I learn, in one way or another, and usually over a good stretch of time, that, all along, with him, I've been deluding myself.

He doesn't want to be friends. He doesn't want to be closer.

I'm not special to him.

Nobody is.

What this person really wants isn't true friendship, true connection, true intimacy. He may think he wants that. And clearly he appears to want it.

But he doesn't.

Why not?

Because, ultimately, what's more important to him than beginning and nurturing true intimacy is protecting himself.

Usually, such people don't utilize friendships to enrich their lives. They use friendships, rather, to insulate themselves from themselves.

They cut off relationships before they can grow into anything deep and real; they don't trust in the nature of love. They may not formally sever a given relationship—they may "remain in the relationship," structurally—but their heart is insulated from and closed to feeding and growing it.

They have, in a real sense, chosen themselves over love. They've chosen to cherish their fears that life—truly living—is threatening, and that love is nothing but dangerous.

Refusing to accept challenges

I once knew a man, "Norman," who was as impressive a person as you could ever meet. He certainly was as impressive a man as I've ever met. Tall; almost ridiculously handsome; in his early years, an accomplished athlete; a successful salesman; beautiful wife, two great kids—and a voice like the best radio announcer ever. (Given my vocation, I have a particular affection for people with voices I can just tell would melt the airwaves. Norman's was as good as any I'd ever heard. He made me sound like Donald Duck. I liked him anyway.)

Plus—and this was one of the most winning things about him— Norman was funny. I don't mean he occasionally cracked the winning joke. Anyone can memorize a line, but you can't learn to be funny in the way he was; he was *born* funny. Beyond this, I think maybe he worked on being funny, too, because he seemed very aware that, if you want someone to buy something, the best thing you can do is get him to laugh.

Through his prowess as a salesman, Norman, in the course of about ten years, turned a relatively small firm into a huge company.

You don't make national business headlines unless someone's buying what you make. And no one buys anything unless someone

74

sells it to them. Norman could sell sand to a bedouin. He had a range of good products to sell, too. He did very well for himself and his family.

As a result, Fortune 500 companies came calling.

When I met him, he had, a year before, become head of sales for one of the largest corporations in the U.S.

Guess what? Norman failed. He could be a salesman, yes: he'd been one his entire life. But it turned out he couldn't, or wouldn't, *manage* salesmen.

"Steve, can you help him?" his lovely wife, Jean, asked. "He won't be a salesman anymore; he says he's absolutely past that phase of his life. But he's *so* unhappy with what he's doing now."

He was. And the more I got to know him, the more I understood why.

Norman was unhappy because he wasn't, in a sense, taking seriously his new opportunities. His position in the firm that had so assiduously courted him entailed doing certain kinds of things—management things—that he simply was not going to do.

Why?

Norman was afraid. He was afraid of public failure. He was afraid of the obstacles facing him. He was afraid the stockholders would never assign credibility to a self-made man "posing as" a corporate titan.

So he failed. Rather than step up to meet the challenges, Norman opted for retirement.

He quit. He walked away.

If you ever find yourself failing at something you thought you really wanted to make successful, ask yourself if there isn't something about your new circumstances or challenges, that, above all, you fear.

Chances are, there will be.

Once you've identified those fears, bring them to God. Show him that you trust him with your well-being.

And then get back in the game. Refusal to see and accept new challenges as open doors for growth demonstrates that you value your own fears above God's assurance that, in truth, you have nothing to fear at all.

You know better than to do that.

(3) How to Give Up Fear

List prominent fears; evaluate how realistic they are

I consider myself very fortunate in that people bring to me, daily, the fears that are interfering with their absolute trust in God. I know I'm blessed to play such a role in their lives. I feel honored that they trust me enough to share with me the difficulties they face in ridding themselves of whatever is keeping them from fully living the abundant life God intends.

If for a long while you do the sort of work people invite me to do, you'll begin to develop certain approaches to the fundamental life-challenges that, through experience, you've learned are most efficacious in taming and outright eliminating the fears that radically compromise healthy living.

One thing I've learned is to ask people to think long and hard about what it is, *exactly*, that they're fearing. I don't ask them simply to ponder what they're afraid of, either; I encourage them to plainly boil down and then list fears. Most of us would do very well to stop having our fears be of a vague, free-floating, essentially mysterious nature and instead make them be clearly defined.

Ninety percent of the time, when people are willing to concentrate on their fears and actually delineate for themselves what they consist of, they find that the things they feared aren't anywhere near as scary as they assumed.

If you sense that your fears are keeping you from the life you know God prefers you to lead, write them down. Don't allow fear to remain threatening from a distance; insist that fears threaten you from right there on the pad in front of you. Note them. Flush them out into the open.

Once you've done that, consider them, one by one.

Are they *really* that scary? If you're suddenly unemployed, will you *actually*, say, lose your home? If you do this thing or that thing, would your parents (or husband or siblings or colleagues) *truly* hate you?

Would you *ultimately* fail? Would you *entirely* end up destitute? *Would your world really end?*

Or, when it's all said and done, are you allowing fear to block you from trusting God?

God *will* make everything okay. That *is* his promise to all who believe on him.

You can let go of your fears. You can trust God. Believe it.

Be okay with some things being truly scary

Nonetheless, some things are going to be frightening.

God is in his heaven, no doubt about it. Someday we'll be there, too.

But for now, we're here. And down here, it's *not* all angels with harps.

———

This morning I made an appointment to see my dentist.

Some people fear spiders. Some fear heights. Some fear spiders on stilts.

Well, my fear is dentists. They cause pain. I don't like the pain they cause. Dentists hurt, and I hate that.

I'm pain-averse. There may be some dentist, somewhere, who knows how to practice without causing the kind of pain that makes patients cringe and, afterward, think they'd rather die of rot than ever make another appointment. But I've never met that dentist. All the ones I've known, no matter how experienced or pedigreed, might as well be going into my mouth with a buzz saw.

Maybe that's a *little* extreme.

Let's say they might as well be trying to fix my teeth with a ball-peen hammer and an ice pick. (By the way, if perchance you're a dentist, please forgive me. I know you're doing your best. If you ever become my tooth-fixer, I'll try my best not to start crying when you pick up a drill.)

In the course of doing their (honorable! important!) work, dentists are going to hurt you. That isn't a negotiable truth. It's like paying taxes. It will happen. In the big picture, there's nothing you can do about it.

If you go to the dentist, you'll suffer. If you don't go to the dentist, you'll suffer. (And so will the people you breathe on.)

That's life. It's what it is. No one can change that.

What's important for the person who's trying not to let her fears interfere with the trust in God she needs to live a truly fulfilling life is to reconcile herself to the truth that it's perfectly okay to fear some things. Trusting in God *doesn't* mean you never fear anything at all. It doesn't mean you're supposed to be fine with, for one example, going to the dentist.

It means that you come to understand the difference between the concerns that naturally are part of this temporal life and the worries that, in light of God's love and God's power, have zero strength or hold over you.

Consider your strengths and adaptability

A friend was recently sharing with me the fear he had that he was getting squeezed out of his job.

"I'm telling you, Steve," he said, "it's happening. I see how it's going. Guys like me, who've been in the field twenty, twenty-five years, cost a lot more money than kids just coming out of college. A kid who's twenty-three, with no wife or kids or anything like that to hold him down, can work sixty hours a week, no problem. And he'll do it for less money than I will.

78

"Sure, that kid doesn't know half of what I do. Sure, my experience will save me from making all kinds of mistakes he couldn't avoid even if he did see them coming—which he never does. But that's not the point, as far as management is concerned. All management wants anymore is the most hours worked they can get for the least amount of money."

"Surely they deeply value your experience, though, don't they?" I asked.

"Yes and no. They know that I know what I'm doing, yes. Yet a lot of what these kids know today is stuff I *don't* know. I can use a computer, sure. But not the way the young people can, with all the social networking and Facebook and Twitter and all that. I don't know anything about that stuff. It makes them seem cool and hip, and makes me seem like a Neanderthal who communicates with grunts and whoops.

"It's really got me worried. I know I'm supposed to trust in God to take care of my finances and well-being and all that. But this is scary. Two guys in my division got laid off just last week—guys who were hired when I was. And they were both real assets to the company. How do I know I'm not next?"

Know what I told my friend? To not be passive toward the thing that's giving him fear.

"Consider your strengths," I encouraged. "*Adapt.*"

So that's what we talked about. Two hours later, he wasn't nearly as afraid of getting fired as he had been. We'd laid out a plan whereby he would marshall his resources, determine what he could do to render himself virtually indispensable, *do* those things, and learn some of the "new stuff" younger people know.

He stopped for a virtual moment. He considered the source of his fears. He thought deeply about the strengths he possessed—the assets and drive that got him to where he was already—and found himself unafraid.

We're to trust in God, yes. Also, sometimes, we can go ahead and trust ourselves, or at least get ourselves moving toward solving the issue at hand.

(4) Gaining Back Trust

Remembering that we all live in God's world

When your trust in God has been eroded or eliminated altogether by your fears, often what you're feeling is that you've somehow stepped into a part of reality that isn't within God's providence, that's outside his protective benevolence. You feel you're dealing with a special set of circumstances, such that you're really and truly threatened by something more powerful than God's ability to protect you from it (or to make it ultimately okay).

In actuality, though, our fears as related to God largely can be illustrated in the same way that fears we might have on any given Disney ride are related to a Disney park on the whole.

Last time I was at Disneyland, I decided to try California Adventure, an immediately adjacent Disney theme park.

I've been to Disneyland a lot; it's one of my favorite places. When I lived on the West Coast, California Adventure, even though it had opened years earlier, never was terribly tempting. If I wanted an adventure, I'd hop in my car and cruise the Pacific Highway. (My whole life, at any rate, was a California Adventure.)

But finally, I gave in. I did at least want to see the Disneyized version of my home state.

Well, there's a ride called the Twilight Zone Tower of Terror, and that pretty much describes it. The "twilight zone" part happens in the lobby of the "hotel" and in the hallways you see as you're sitting on a platform that rises, and rises, and rises. The "terror" part happens when, having reached the top of the 199-foot-tall structure, you freefall, all the way to just before the ground.

I screamed like a little girl. In fact, I screamed more than the little girl (Madeline, my daughter) sitting next to me.

You know what happened right there, for a panic-striken, almost-199-foot moment? I forgot I was in the happiest place on earth—or at least a place built by the same people who'd built the happiest place on earth, next door.

I forgot. My fears were stronger than my sense of trust.

When the ride ended and I walked back out into the sunshine that even the Imagineers couldn't possibly imagine how to create, I remembered that I was, after all, in Disney territory.

I was fine. Everything was okay.

Next time you find yourself too afraid to trust God, just ask yourself whether or not you're still in God's world.

Remembering that God is good and watching out for you

Not too long ago I was at the beach with a friend, Mike, and his two young children. Mike's daughter, Janey, is ten, and as cute as she can be. One of the things I liked most about our time that day was watching what great care Janey took of her little brother, Philip, who's six.

While Mike and I sat in lawn chairs, watching them and chatting, Janey and Philip played in the ocean. Janey, proficient in the water, went out further than did her brother.

Like any kid, Philip was just thrilled to be splashing about. But sometimes the strength of the receding waves would drag him out into the water a bit farther than he wanted to go; other times, without noticing, he'd be having so much fun with newfound friends that he wouldn't see how far out he'd gone. He never went anywhere near a depth that was dangerous for him. You could see, though, that he wasn't quite as sure of this as Mike and I were.

Philip would be getting knocked aside by a playful wave, or spiritedly dog-paddling (of which he was already quite the master), when suddenly he would look around, frightened. Very often, the first place he looked was toward Janey. Surely one of the best big sisters any kid ever had, she always was near enough that he was comforted and reassured. He'd appear a bit panicked, spin around, spot Janey nearby . . . and you could see his little body relax. Then he'd go right back to having fun.

And whenever Janey found herself a little farther from shore than she expected to be, to whom do you think *she* looked? Janey's an outstanding swimmer, and while, again, she never ventured so far it could prove truly problematic, she did sometimes find herself with reason to be sure that, if need be, her father was close enough to rescue her.

And of course, he was. Sometimes Mike would get up and go stand in the water, just to ensure Janey knew he was there, watching out for her.

Just as Philip looked for assurance from Janey, and Janey from Mike, so we should remember that though sometimes we may feel we're in too deep, we have only to look to Jesus, who never leaves the shore and never takes his eyes from us. He's always there, always ready to help us back to solid footing.

Remembering God's promise for your future

Of all the gifts God has given us through the miracle of Jesus Christ, none is more glorious and precious than eternal life. What could possibly compare? There isn't a single thing we could obtain that would be better than, or worth anywhere near as much as, what God has promised us after we walk this earth no more.

However, the assurance of God Almighty that from the moment we pass into the next life we'll live forever in his presence doesn't seem to me, somehow, to mean as much to most Christians as I'd think it would.

I don't mean that believers I've known don't care about God's gift; certainly they do. And I'm not suggesting they're unaware of this most important divine guarantee, either. I know that's not true. I'd venture to guess that every believer I've ever met knows about God-pledged afterlife glories.

Most of us grew up learning all about heaven in Sunday school. There might have been a lot about the Bible that they *didn't* teach us there (probably for the best; I still blush when I read certain Old Testament passages), but Christ's assurance of everlasting life definitely wasn't omitted. That's something just about every kid who's ever spent a single morning at church is bound to know.

Remember John 10:28? "I give them eternal life, and they will never perish. No one can snatch them away from me." And who could forget John 3:16? "God loved the world so much that he gave his one and only Son, so that everyone who believes in him will not perish but have eternal life."

Right? You can't even watch a football game without seeing the giant "John 3:16" sign that's usually behind the end zone. (I often wonder if the kicker, being familiar with that verse, shanks a field goal or has his extra point blocked and then goes, "Oh well. At least I have everlasting life.")

We know God has promised us *forever*. Yet too many of us fail to let that thought—that reality!—sink deep down enough to once and for all obliterate our nagging fears. What do we have to fear, in this life, if *eternity* is ours?

The key to gaining back the trust you need to live a life filled with God's best is just this: to realize that God's best for you hasn't even started yet.

(5) Living a Life Filled With Trust

Boldly living

As I contemplated how and why it is that a man who's fully trusting in God lives boldly, I realized something about myself that I've never known until this very moment.

That's a big part of why I write. While I take a downright sublime pleasure in helping to teach others, in the process I also learn things about myself that I might not discover in any other way. Right now I'm having one of those moments.

The insight is that I don't want on my headstone the words, "He loved well." (Not even sure what exactly that means. I only know I don't want people hanging around my grave, trying to figure it out.) Or "He was a good man" (boring, vague). Or "An exceptional driver" (not true anyway). Or definitely any sort of epitaph that's typical.

None of those. I want people to remember about me, "He lived *boldly*."

What better testimony could there be to a person's character?

It's one thing to be bold. Anybody can be bold. It's a very different thing altogether to *live* boldly.

The only kind of person who lives boldly is the one who's unafraid. And the only kind of person who's unafraid of everything is one who puts his complete, utter trust in the Lord.

Here's a prayer for you and me, right now:

Lord, let me live boldly. Let me cease to worry constantly that I'm not good enough, not intelligent enough, not well enough prepared or equipped.

Take all such fears from me, Lord, and let me instead be filled with the strength, power, and confidence of knowing that nothing in this world can hurt me as long as I trust in what you've promised me in the next.

Let me be forthright, not hesitant. Let me be direct, not circumspect. Let me be brave, not cowardly. Let me skip with joy into situations that, were I to forget you, would surely have me tiptoeing with fear.

Let me, Lord, live boldly, from now until the moment I'm with you. Amen.

Empowering others

I don't have lots of talents. I do a few things pretty well, and with most of the rest I manage well enough to at least fool some of the people some of the time. But if there's one significant life skill to which I can lay claim without many, if any, of those who know me screaming foul, it's that I know how to empower others. (Or, perhaps better said, I know how to get out of the way and allow people to apply their own God-given talents and strengths.)

I *live* to empower others. It's the greatest thing there is for me to do. Whether I'm ministering to an attendee who's finally giving up the addiction that's been burdening him and his family for years, or a caller who wants to start connecting with her husband rather than scolding him, it makes me feel wonderful to know I've empowered a person to take one step closer to fulfilling his or her God-instilled potential.

And of all the things I love about this, best of all is empowering the people I work with. The truth is, while I do love delegating and assigning real responsibilities to those who must do their job well in order for New Life to be everything it can be, I'm still a bit of a control freak. It's not actually natural for me to take an important aspect of our work and trust someone else to do it right.

It's for this very reason that I love doing it! It's the surest way I have, every single day, of putting my trust in others ahead of my fear of things going wrong. Instead of finding it worrisome to empower someone in my organization to venture outside her comfort zone, or to add something to what he's accustomed to, I find it invigorating. It's fun. It feels like what it really is: *a leap of faith.*

I think sometimes we make showing our trust in God a little harder than it needs to be, insofar as the opportunities for doing it aren't exactly hidden. They're everywhere. A chance to demonstrate how much you trust God—which is to say, how much you love God— usually is no further away than whoever, at any given moment, happens to be standing right beside you.

Living optimistically

I know a man who could depress the Teletubbies. He's a good guy. I like him.

85

One thing I like most about "Lonny" is that he's funny. But his humor is definitely of the gallows variety: all Lonny's jokes—well, his snarky asides and sardonic observations; he doesn't tell "jokes"— seem to have at their core a conviction that nothing ever goes (or will go) right.

Lonny almost never says anything nice about anything at all without following up, right away, with something to undercut the pleasant or flattering thing he just said.

"That's a nice shirt you're wearing. I remember when those were in fashion."

"Sure enjoyed seeing the Lakers the other night. Of course, I couldn't *see* them at all; I was sitting behind a pillar. The game *sounded* great, though."

"Watched a really good movie Friday. Can't remember the name. Doesn't really matter, though, does it—they're all the same."

I was with Lonny once when a mutual friend, a younger man, shared with the two of us that he'd just purchased his first home.

"Congratulations," I said. "That's wonderful! You're going to love being a homeowner."

"You will," added Lonny. "It's great. Nothing like having your own place. Of course, miss *one* payment and you'll find out who *really* owns it."

You get the idea. He's like Eeyore, but edgier.

Lonny doesn't mean anyone any harm. However, he's also an example of what many of us too often allow ourselves to become: a profound pessimist.

Lonny's good at turning a gloomy outlook into humor; he has a charming way of delivering downer comments that tends to dull the bite of his actual statements. But at heart, he chronically sees *nothing* as truly good or pure.

At heart, Lonny's afraid. Words are his self-defense against being hurt.

If you never expect anything, you're never disappointed, right?

But you also never hope. And as we've seen, people never live well without hope.

Don't be like Lonny. Live optimistically. Believe in the joy that God is waiting for you to receive as your birthright!

Be boldly optimistic. Let yourself be hope-filled, hope*ful*.

This is, in the end, the only natural response to God.

Questions for Discussion

1. What would you say, right now, is the biggest fear in your life? Why?

2. We've talked about the connection between loving God and trusting God. Do you think it's possible to love God without fully trusting him? Do you think you ever love God more than you trust him?

3. How big a role do you think God's promise of eternal salvation plays in your everyday life? In the course of your day, what sorts of things make you forget the heaven that awaits you as a believer?

4. Talk about a fear you once had that turned out to be much greater than the thing that was generating the fear.

5. Is there anything you desire that you know your fears are keeping you from doing or pursuing? How realistic do you think those fears are?

6. Do you have a Lonny in your life? How do you respond to his negativity and pessimism? Does it affect your mood or outlook at all?

4

Give Up Anger; Get Back Forgiveness

(1) What Is Anger?

Deeper, more subtle than you might think

Whenever I think of someone having trouble controlling or process-ing their anger, I always recall the angriest classic cartoon character: the ever-furious, ever-sputtering, ever-flapping Donald Duck.

Now that's one angry duck-person. And it's easy enough to as-sociate the kind of demonstrative fury ol' Donald evinces at the drop of a sailor's cap with actions typical of type-A folks. That's why we love Donald: we recognize him in people.

I wish we didn't. I wish it weren't so easy to recognize ourselves and/or others in Donald Duck's outrageous behavior. Wouldn't it be great if he *weren't* so famous and beloved? If nobody understood what that character was about, if nobody thought it believable that any creature (even a duck!) would ever be that angry all the time, would we so easily throw fits as wildly over-the-top as those regularly thrown by *The* Donald? Wouldn't it be good if, when he launched into another indecipherable tirade, instead of laughing, people simply looked at each other and said, "I don't get it—is this supposed to be funny? What's that duck's *problem*?"

But that's not the case. We laugh because in the histrionics we do completely recognize ourselves or others. (Usually others, right? It's *others* who rant and rave, *others* who can't seem to manage their temper, *others* who should be embarrassed to act "that way" when they get ticked off. Bosses, husbands, Beverly Hills housewives, football coaches, essentially insane people of every sort and ilk—*they* have obvious anger issues.)

Here's the thing that's too easy to forget when considering what anger does, doesn't, or might mean in your life: the kind of fury Donald Duck displays—livid, unbridled, take-no-prisoners rage—is to regular, everyday, low-level anger what a roaring forest fire is to the flame of a match.

Yes, they're of the same substance. And yes, a candle-flame can easily enough become an out-of-control blaze. Little flickers, though, are a lot more common than all-consuming barn burners.

The crazed tantrum you might occasionally throw *isn't* emblematic of the anger that's maybe getting between you and the God-centered, God-generated forgiveness you need to live the godly life you most want to lead.

That sort of obvious rage would be easy to identify and deal with.

The kind of anger most of us carry around, the kind that often damages our relationships with others, burns much, much deeper. It's usually a subtle, glowing "thing" that's slowly but surely burning a hole right through us.

Creates impatience, negative assumptions

The weird thing about anger is that, more than any other emotion, it readily disguises itself as all kinds of stuff it's not.

When I was young, I worked for the most impatient person I think I've ever known, and certainly for whom I've ever worked. Out of respect for him or her, I won't be too specific; my job was to help "Chris" do Chris's job.

Many people worked for Chris, who had a powerful position in the company that employed us. I was privileged to be Chris's number one assistant. Whenever Chris wanted something done, I did it myself or got busy finding the proper person to do it.

When employees saw Chris coming, they suddenly found themselves something to do that required all concentration. Heads would go down; hands would get busy; feet would get moving. People would remember something extremely important in a location across the building. Walking around headquarters with Chris was like ambling through a store with a skunk by the tail. Everybody got the heck out of there.

I liked Chris. Chris spoke to me differently than to anyone else there. Everyone who worked underneath Chris (which was just about everybody) found Chris pretty harsh: dismissive, brusque, condescending. Nobody's work was ever quite good enough. Chris just wasn't a very warm person.

But toward me, Chris was fairly gentle. And this always surprised me. Whenever Chris and I were alone, the first thing I felt was nervous; I never wanted Chris to turn on me the same general tone Chris adopted with others. This never seemed to happen, though—when it was just the two of us, Chris would become calm and often thoughtful; reflective, even.

One day, alone with me in Chris's office, Chris said, "People don't like me, do they? I see it, you know. I can tell they don't like me."

"Oh, I wouldn't say that," I responded, gingerly.

"Don't kid a kidder. I know people don't like me." Then Chris began spilling Chris's guts.

Chris talked for about an hour straight. It was a remarkable experience; I hadn't expected anything like that to happen. Chris always

91

seemed so self-contained, so confident, so *not* inclined to emotional bonding. Yet here Chris was, pouring out Chris's heart.

And do you know what Chris, right there, told me the problem was?

"I'm just so *angry*," Chris suddenly gushed, with tears in both eyes. "I don't even know why—or at whom, really. But it's with me always, this anger. I think this is the first time I've ever realized that's exactly what it is: anger." Chris looked at me, defeated, yet also—I could see—excited and relieved to have, unexpectedly (it seemed), come into the truth.

That's when I first realized: anger doesn't always look like anger. I'd never thought of Chris as particularly angry. Impatient, yes. Pretty intolerant, check. Unsentimental, absolutely. But not specifically *angry*.

And I saw then something that's been reaffirmed daily as I've watched and listened to others: anger *rarely* looks like pure, simple anger. What it looks like, often, is a "negative" personality trait of one strain or another: pessimism, anxiety, defeatism, arrogance.

What this taught me—and what, again, people have affirmed for me every day since that talk with Chris—is that anger lies at our very deepest "level." It has to go through a lot of filters, twists, and turns before it finally manifests out in the open of a personality.

Most of the time, people don't even realize that what's really fueling much of their dysfunction is pure anger. When they *do* realize this—boy, can the sun ever start shining in their lives.

Months after that fateful talk, Chris told me that right there, in the office with me, was the first time Chris had ever gotten on Chris's knees and prayed.

Always looking for fault and culpability

Have you ever known someone whose first instinct, whenever anything around him goes wrong, is to quickly assign blame—and inevitably, of course, to someone, *anyone*, but himself—for that wrong?

June, a woman with whom I used to work, was smart, more than capable of handling her responsibilities. She had a great personality, too: she laughed readily and always had something warm and folksy to say.

But June had a habit that wasn't anything you'd call generally helpful. She *instantly* would absolve herself of *any* and *all* blame for *anything* that went wrong *anywhere near* her range of duties. Further, what raised to something of an art form the alacrity with which she did this was how seamlessly she combined the declaration of her innocence with the pinning of fault on another warm body.

It never failed. Plus, it's one of those things that, as you start paying attention, you really notice. Once I began to comprehend that virtually nothing, ever, was June's "fault"—and especially, it seemed, the things that very clearly were—I couldn't help but note how, each time, she adroitly established her own clearance and simultaneously assigned a different person's culpability.

"Oh, that's something I told Martin to do. Guess he just forgot."

"I remember asking Carl to follow up. Thought he heard me—but apparently not."

"I *knew* Deb was going to get that wrong. I should've said something."

And on and on. She had a million of 'em.

June was broken. Her singular obsession with directly absolving herself and, sometimes less directly, positing the failure of others was like a hairline crack around the circumference of a china teapot. That is, whether or not you notice it right away, the faultline means the pot's at real risk. It needs "fixing," or healing, before something traumatic happens.

I made an effort to get to know June better. Over the months, as she and I talked, I came to see that she was carrying around a busload of deep-seated anger. It was disguised, yes: as I say, June was a very personable woman. But she was angry, and her anger didn't have a natural way to express itself.

Anger's like boiling water. It *will* escape upward—or, if constrained, it will keep building and building pressure. Something's gotta give.

I'm happy to say that today June no longer is inclined to avoid and assign blame. With a little therapy and a lot of prayer, she came to understand that, in persistently defending herself while assigning fault elsewhere, she'd been trying to gain for herself the love and affirmation she'd always craved (but had rarely received) from her parents.

Anger flows within us in some very deep waters. Look at the negative traits in your own behavior, no matter how small or minor they might seem.

This or that "symptom" might just be steam, escaping.

(2) What Anger Does to Your Life

Turns you into a judge

If there's one thing you can say about anger, it's that anger is extremely unpleasant to experience. It *hurts*. There's no fun in being angry all the time.

But if you're a person who's carrying around a whole lot of unresolved anger, what can you do about it? You don't want to *feel* it, that's for sure. Who voluntarily walks up to a grill and grabs a bunch of hot coals to keep in his pocket? No one. Because that would hurt.

And it wouldn't actually be that different from feeling the white-hot anger constantly boiling inside. At least the pain from the coals eventually would go away. The pain of seething anger, though—that really sticks around.

It's probably been with you, after all, for a long, long while.

Since you don't want to directly experience the anger, what are you going to do?

Well, you might do what a few have done when their anger seems too much to deal with. You might become a judge.

Judges know everything. It's their *job* to know everything. A judge is in full command of all the information before her. She has power over the entire arena in which everything before her happens. She's the arbiter. Her say, in many regards, is final.

The judge knows all.

As it happens, that's a handy perspective to adapt, too, if what you're trying to *avoid* knowing is something that's extremely important to you. What does an angry person do as she's becoming someone who coolly passes judgment on everything and everyone? She provides for herself *a means of staying detached.*

Judges aren't personally vested in the conditions, actions, and people they judge. They're not supposed to be impassioned about what they judge. Conversely, they're cool. They're calm. They're reasoned.

They're above it all.

If you go through life judging everyone and everything, think for a moment about what you're really doing. The chances are outstanding that by setting yourself up with an uncompromising opinion on anything you come across, you're using megawatts of energy to avoid the anger inside—anger toward which, in fact, you're anything but detached.

Catch yourself the next time you find yourself declaring judgment. If your personality is "the classic judge's," that time won't be long in coming.

Stop yourself, in midthought or in midsentence.

Consider, very hard, that thing about which you're passing judgment.

Now, ask yourself, with all of your heart, how much you really care about that thing.

I'd bet my house the answer will be *not one bit.*

You don't care about it.

You're using it to distract you from what you care about more than anything else in the world.

Keeps others wary of you

There's nothing intrinsically wrong with anger. Some anger is good; if we weren't angry at things that are wrong, where would we ever get the energy to fix them?

> When they arrived back in Jerusalem, Jesus entered the Temple and began to drive out the people buying and selling animals for sacrifices. He knocked over the tables of the money changers and the chairs of those selling doves, and he stopped everyone from using the Temple as a marketplace.
>
> He said to them, "The Scriptures declare, 'My Temple will be called a house of prayer for all nations,' but you have turned it into a den of thieves."
>
> When the leading priests and teachers of religious law heard what Jesus had done, they began planning how to kill him. But they were afraid of him because the people were so amazed at his teaching.
>
> —Mark 11:15–18

Was Jesus having a problem with his anger? Heck no! He was making sure *other* people had a problem with his anger. This was a righteous anger—that is, he was angry for the right reason—and it was in righteousness that he acted upon it.

What else is Jesus doing here? *Engaging* those money changers and sellers. *Confronting* them, telling them exactly why they'd so enraged him.

He wasn't keeping them at a distance. He was right up in their faces.

That's what you do when you're in touch with your anger. You use it. You act on it. You apply your energy to the pursuit of a right, just result.

But if a person is out of touch with anger—if he's not really aware of what he's mad at, or why—then he learns to behave in ways that merely keep others wary. He doesn't give positive, purposeful emphasis to his emotion. He doesn't channel it toward anything beneficial. Mainly, he's just wasting fuel.

We've all known people so flat-out hostile that, whenever possible, we avoid them. We know that if we engage, we're going to regret it; they're going to make us pay the price for venturing within their sphere of reaction. So we keep our distance. We take the long way around.

What's decidedly tragic is, those who routinely act in ways that guarantee others will remain across the electric fence (or razor wire) very often are puzzled that no one wants to hang out with them. Many are like snapping dogs who wonder why they never get attention or affection.

They don't see that their hostility (and they're probably not even seeing the hostility itself) is keeping almost everyone else at bay.

My advice: look at your own life. Do you make people feel welcomed to talk with you? Do they go out of their way to be with you?

Do you have friends? Do you get invited places?

Do you take pleasure in the company of others? Do they take pleasure in being with you?

If not—if you're lonely, isolated, without a network of friends upon whom you can depend, and whom you're sure love you as much as you love them—then please, consider that the reason is no mystery at all. Seriously ponder the idea that, through actions and words, you're keeping others wary.

Chances are you're not doing that because you're mad at everybody in the world. You're doing it because you sense that you can't really be mad at the only people with whom, deep down, you're truly angry.

Blocks your view of the big picture

"I can't stand working with that guy!" M. huffed. She was CFO at the company for which I worked.

"Really?" I said. I knew we had some problems with this particular co-worker of hers, but I didn't know it was as bad as she apparently thought. "What's wrong?"

"What's *right*? The man's a disaster! I don't even know what he *does* for a living."

"He's our development director."

"I know what's on his business card. I know what he's *supposed* to be doing. I *know* we're paying him a ton of money to do it. It's just that he's *not*. He doesn't do any development. He does zero outreach. He hasn't established that big speaker's panel he said he would. He isn't reaching out to donors. He doesn't even take care of the donors we have. He's basically stopped mailing thank-you letters to those who've taken our cause to heart and actually donated money. Don't you think people who give to us deserve some sort of thanks from us?" Veins were starting to show on her forehead.

"Yes, I do," I answered.

"Well, they're not getting any. I asked him what happened to thank-you notes, and do you know how he answered? *He doesn't have any printed envelopes!* I said, 'Well, order some! Print out our return address yourself!' Hasn't the guy ever used a pen? Or would we have to hire him an assistant for that, too?"

"C'mon, now, though," I urged. "It's not like—"

"And what does he actually *do* on our two big fund-raisers anymore? If he's not going to *do* development, shouldn't he at least do the *other* thing he's responsible for? Shouldn't the fund-raising be something he *does*? Yet it's not! He acts like the events are so unbelievably burdensome that he's carrying the whole world on his shoulders—but if you look at the work he himself has to do for those events to come off right, it's just about *nothing*. Between what you do yourself, Steve, and what our volunteers do, about the only thing left for him is to walk around moaning and complaining about how much work he has. Who does he think he's kidding with that act?"

The more M. complained, the more I started realizing: she was letting her anger and frustration with our development director (who, to be sure, was having problems) blind her to the broader truth. Her own work had been slipping lately, and as she vented and ranted, it was clear why: she was spending so much time tracking the DD's output that she wasn't giving enough attention to her own.

In minding someone else's business, she was failing to mind hers.

And we all do that, don't we? We let anger become a funnel for restricting our view of the whole reality. We obsess so much over one thing that we become impaired in our perception of everything else around it.

It's good to be aware of problems, and to address them. Nobody should argue that. But if you find you have issues that trigger inner fury and foaming hostility, do yourself a favor. Pull back. Take a deep breath. *Look at the bigger picture.*

It's likely you'll discover that the problem seems so big because you're looking at it too closely.

(3) How to Give Up Anger

Freeze-frame and examine your angry moments

One element that makes anger so compelling is that it always feels so justified. Somebody says something mean, or does something so wrong you half expect God's giant hand to descend from the sky and flick his forehead, and your anger attaches itself to that guy like a frog's long tongue on a fat, lazy fly.

He's wrong. You're right. And you're angry. That's the way it is.

This little internal exchange happens . . . how many times a day? Ten? Twenty? Thirty?

Well, guess what. There's a game you can play the next time you feel angry at what someone has done or said. I like to call it, "Surprise: It's You!"

Simple rules: the next time you get angry at someone, stop.

Just stop. Freeze your mind in place. Forget whatever offense triggered your hostility; it'll still be there when you get back. Lock your mind, right where it is.

Then, look at your mind. See how it's really thinking; consider what it's truly doing. Let your mind tell you what's actually going on with it.

With a moment or two of patience, if you keep your mind "in the moment" at which you stopped it, it will reveal to you all kinds of goings-on that, had you rushed into your next thought, you wouldn't have noticed.

It's like pausing an epic film—as if you took, say, a frame from the *Gone With the Wind* scene showing all the wounded soldiers lying about in the Atlanta rail yard, and stopped it. The more you examined that single, crystal-clear "moment" on-screen, the more you'd see. You'd notice a lot more detail than you'd ever process with the camera panning across those fighters.

If you stop the movie frame in your head when it's playing the intense short feature *I'm Angry Now,* do you know what, nine in ten times, you'll see?

That you're not truly angry with *that* person at all.

Oh, you'd still have a problem with whatever it is she did or said. No doubt about it. But guess what your real issue would be with whatever she did or said, or didn't do or say?

The actual issue is that it touched a nerve in you. What "she did" angered you not because of how objectively errant it was but because in it you saw a reflection of an inadequacy you think *you* have.

She reminded you of something about yourself that you're very sensitive about being reminded of.

Anger, truly, is rarely about the other person at all. It's usually about something that's wrong—or (most often) you think is wrong—with you.

Realize how much anger works against you

One aspect that makes anger such a difficult emotion to handle is how seductive it is. It pulls you in; it grabs all your attention; it compels you, if only for a moment, to care more about it than about anything else. When you're angry at something, you tend to be *really* angry at it. Even if only in passing, for that moment you tend to be fully, 100-percent angry.

You know how it is. You're on a corner, ready to cross the street. You've pushed the button; you're watching the light. You're doing what you're supposed to do (stand at the curb and wait your turn).

The light finally changes. You step out—and some *jerk* making a rushed right turn shoots *just* by you instead of doing what *he's* supposed to do (wait).

Practically runs you over!

In that instant, if you could get your hands around that moron's neck, you'd strangle him. Then you'd curse him. You'd slash his tires. You'd jump up and down on the stupid hood of his stupid car until it caved.

You'd give him a *piece of your mind.*

But you know what? By being so angry at that driver, you did give him a piece of your mind. That's what actually happened. Thoughts you could have been pondering, energy you could have been extending out into the world, anything godlike that might have been going on in your soul was, in a whoosh, snatched away.

The more accurate truth is, you didn't give his careless thoughtlessness just a piece of your mind. You gave all of it.

This means your mind didn't belong to you. It wasn't yours to do with as you chose. You lost control of it.

Anger almost always works against you—especially the transitory, sharp anger that surges up and flashes. Such anger is bad for your heart, bad for your chemistry, bad for your circulation, bad for your mood.

It's bad for your relationship with God. How can you think about God—how can you be with him, listen to him, respond to him, pray to him—if your mind has fully attached itself to something that's out of your control anyway?

You can't.

And you won't.

Until you replace your anger toward that driver with the forgiveness you *can* right away extend to him (by the way, God, through Jesus, certainly has shown how far he's willing to go to show his forgiveness to you), your anger will continue to work against you in ways you'll never even know about.

Take inventory of anger's cost

I have a friend, "Dean," whose best friend had an affair with his wife. During the course of their adultery Dean's once-dear friend and once-beloved wife both lied to him, for what Dean later learned was almost a year.

When Dean found out what had been happening, he exploded. He went ballistic. He ranted; he raved; he screamed; he hurled objects against the walls: in every way, Dean took his terrible discovery about as hard as you'd expect from someone who's just realized a betrayal of such magnitude.

In his telling of the story, it sounded to me like when he found out what was going on, Dean almost killed one or the other of them. He didn't go that far, thank God. But it seemed he came pretty close.

Matter of fact, I think Dean's ex-friend and ex-wife think he came near to doing that, too. Dean wasn't through even half his rage when they hightailed it together right out of town, fleeing as though they were running for their lives. As I say, they might very well have been.

That Dean was so angry over what had happened is perfectly normal. Of course, it's not normal for any man to have to discover about his life what Dean did—but his *reaction* was reasonable to expect. Yes, he sort of lost his mind. Who wouldn't?

The problem with Dean, however, is that even though he experienced this horrendous misfortune four years ago, he's still so furious with his ex-wife and ex-friend that it's practically sucked every joule of energy from his life. It's about all he ever thinks about. *If,* for a few minutes at a time, Dean talks of anything else, it's never long at all until he redirects the entire conversation back to the subject of what happened when the love of his life ran off with one of the best pals he's ever had.

Dean was failing to let go of his anger over the wrong once done to him. So, know what I did? I sat him down, and rather than saying, essentially, to get over it, I suggested that, for one whole day, he write down the time whenever he found himself thinking or talking about his wrecked marriage.

"Carry a notepad," I said, "and jot down the moment when you realize you're doing it again. Do this whether or not you thought about it angrily."

"Oh, I'll be angry," said Dean. "But all right. I'll do it."

He did. At the end of the day, do you know what he realized when he saw what must have been a hundred times listed on his pad? The betrayal, which had destroyed his life four years ago, was destroying it still.

In the present, Dean is beyond his anger. Once he had an objective means of measuring just how intrusive and even ruinous his old anger was in and for his current life, Dean took the necessary steps to bring perspective back into balance. He started seeing a counselor. He started attending church regularly.

Slowly but surely, Dean regained his God-given ability to forgive.

You can do the same. If you have a sense that your anger is costing more than you'd like to keep paying, jot down the times, throughout one whole day, when you feel yourself experiencing anger. At day's end, look at that list.

This is your anger inventory.

What does any business do with far more inventory than it needs? Dumps it.

(4) Gaining Back Forgiveness

Remembering how forgiving Jesus was

Two other men, both criminals, were also led out with him to be executed. When they came to the place called the Skull, they crucified him there, along with the criminals—one on his right, the other on his left. Jesus said, "Father, forgive them, for they do not know what they are doing." And they divided up his clothes by casting lots.

The people stood watching, and the rulers even sneered at him. They said, "He saved others; let him save himself if he is God's Messiah, the Chosen One."

The soldiers also came up and mocked him. They offered him wine vinegar and said, "If you are the king of the Jews, save yourself."

There was a written notice above him, which read: THIS IS THE KING OF THE JEWS.

One of the criminals who hung there hurled insults at him: "Aren't you the Messiah? Save yourself and us!"

But the other criminal rebuked him. "Don't you fear God," he said, "since you are under the same sentence? We are punished justly, for we are getting what our deeds deserve. But this man has done nothing wrong."

Then he said, "Jesus, remember me when you come into your kingdom."

Jesus answered him, "Truly I tell you, today you will be with me in paradise."

—Luke 23:32–43, NIV

If ever anyone has had a reason to be righteously and fearfully angry, surely it was Jesus on the cross.

Has anyone been treated worse? More heinously, in comparison to what he deserves?

No.

But at the height of his agony, at the very pinnacle of his suffering, what does Jesus say? What does he pronounce?

"I forgive. They don't even understand what they're actually doing."

To whom is Jesus offering his forgiveness? The soldiers crucifying him? The spectators just watching? The mockers cheering on the murder?

Whom does Jesus implore God in heaven to forgive?

All of them. Each of them. Everyone.

Us.

The anger we harbor in our hearts blocks us from being able to forgive. It freezes our will to love, robs us of our God-given impetus to absolve. In our heart we know we should allow forgiving love to reign, not unforgiving anger. We want to be people who don't let anger get the better of them, who have the capacity, at any given moment, to substitute the healing power of God's love for the hateful feelings of rage and revenge that sweep through us.

We do. That's what we want. That's the kind of person we fervently desire either to be or to become.

Time and time again, though, we utterly fail to become anywhere near that righteous. Despite our impassioned efforts to rise above the fray, we consistently sink right back down into it.

Before we can stop ourselves, we choose anger over forgiveness— or, more precisely, we prove helpless as anger, with so little effort on its part, once again chooses us.

And there is Jesus, in horrific agony, proclaiming nothing but forgiveness for the very people doing him unimaginable harm. He doesn't ask God to stop the hands of the killers. He doesn't send a lightning bolt to smite those he knows won't stop until his holy spirit is violently separated from his corporeal body. He doesn't annihilate each and every person within five miles of Calvary.

He forgives.

What better model could we have as we seek the strength to forgive?

Clearly, that's Jesus' primary message to us through his death: forgive.

Forgive, forgive, forgive.

He wants nothing higher from us. Nothing higher exists.

Turn away from your anger, and fix your eyes on the cross.

Forgiving others as Jesus forgave you

I prefer not to have the only people I associate with be Christian. I love my believing brothers and sisters and, of course, have much in common with them. But I know that if I don't spend time among those with perspectives and belief systems other than mine, I'll never grow. I'll never learn what things look like for those who live their lives, or at least understand the context in which they live their lives, in ways that foundationally differ from mine.

One such person I admire deeply, a man I'll call Dale, took a job on the other side of the map. Almost right before he left, he said to me (suddenly, one day, as we were sitting on a park bench overlooking the Pacific), "I like your Christianity, Steve. I really do. And I think I could get on board with it. Jesus is such an admirable, compelling figure. But I don't get the part about how he died for me *personally*. It's the personal part—the part about Jesus being my *personal* Savior—that I really just can't understand."

I had to say I understood his dilemma. The God of the universe, the Creator of all things big and small—this God is easier for me to fathom. Even God the Maker of me. But the truly personal part—for God to want to be close to every person, to desire a relationship with each one—is a bit of a stretch.

The stretch is always longer when I'm full of anger and resentment. When I'm free of it, though, it's much easier to accept God's forgiveness personally and seek personal connection and intimacy with him.

As I consider that anyone aiming to give up anger to get back forgiveness can't do better than turning to Christ as the ultimate model, I think of how important it is to realize, with all of our heart, that Jesus forgave each and every one of us *personally*. The very fact of his forgiveness being so personal bestows upon us all the power we'd ever need to personally forgive others.

As we get from Jesus, so we give.

If my friend ever reads this, I want him to hear the following:

Hi, Dale.

How do you like Ohio? Finding good things there? Call me!

More to the point: if you really want to understand the dynamic whereby Christ died on the cross for your personal sins, to save your personal soul, the best thing is to pray. Close your eyes, think of God, ask him to reveal to you anything about Jesus that he sees fit.

What I'm hoping you then receive, Dale, is the Holy Spirit of Jesus Christ himself. Because if you do, you'll know, right then and there, virtually everything there is to know about your relationship to him, and about how he won, for you, eternal salvation. That's what you need to know if you want to understand how you're personally saved.

If you want the darkness that is life outside of Christ to lift—if you want to walk in the sun of everlasting victory rather than continue making your way without the guiding light of his love—then you, my friend, need Jesus. You must receive into your heart what Jesus offers you through his sacrificial atonement.

And don't forget to call me. Or write!

If *you* are struggling to accept in full the truth that Jesus has forgiven *you*, then do as I've suggested to Dale. *Pray.* Pray that Jesus delivers you from the anger that's preventing you from being able to love and forgive others the way he loves and has forgiven you.

You cannot withhold your forgiveness if you truly believe that God, through Jesus, has forgiven you.

What's really causing you, though, to fail at forgiving isn't even your anger. It's much more simple, and much more intimate, than that. The truth is, you don't think God loves you as much as he truly does.

You don't really believe you fully deserve the forgiveness of Jesus. But because of what Jesus did, you *do*. God did die for *you*!

If you doubt it, you know what to do.

Take that doubt, put it in your hands, and lay it at the foot of the cross. Jesus will take care of the rest.

(5) Living a Life Filled With Forgiveness

To err is human

When you forgive somebody, what are you really saying to her? What's the message you're truly conveying? You're acknowledging that, honestly, in a fundamental sense, you (or "we") are no different than she (or "they").

Yes, she may have done something about which she should feel remorse. Yes, she might well have hurt you, and deeply. Chances are she *did*, or there wouldn't be anything for you to forgive.

She did mess up. She did wrong. She did act selfishly. She did put herself first. In whatever specific way she transgressed against you, the bottom line is you're justified in your anger toward her. She deserves it. She's earned your wrath or indignation.

However. If you walk with Christ, then you know: having the prerogative to withhold forgiveness toward someone who's done you wrong doesn't mean it's okay if you do. It's very definitely not okay not to forgive others as Christ forgives you. In real and practical terms, you are to do as Christ himself did whenever he was wronged or maligned or disrespected.

Love. Forgive.

The key to doing that—to losing your anger and forgiving—is remembering that you *are* just like the person you need to forgive.

Isn't that the funniest thing? The key to emulating Christ isn't to imagine being him or to act so much like him that you approximate his holiness. It's almost the opposite! In the triad between you, Jesus, and the person in the wrong, the one you're most like—practically identical to—is the other guy.

Sure, he wronged you. But would you even dare to suggest you've never wronged another person at least as egregiously? Are you going to pretend you've never hurt anyone as much as he's hurt you?

Of course you wouldn't. You know better. You know that's what people do. They mess up. They act selfishly. They take what isn't theirs and then try to blame someone else for what's missing.

People do all kinds of things they shouldn't do.

And so do you.

To err, as "they" say, is human.

The person who hurt you isn't your enemy. He is your brother.

It's relaxing to forgive others!

Remember Bobby McFerrin's "Don't Worry, Be Happy"? I was fascinated when that tune became a phenomenally popular hit a couple decades ago. You could tell people loved its sublimely catchy melody even more than the song itself.

As an ongoing student of human spirituality, I found myself extremely curious about what exactly it was with "Don't Worry, Be Happy" that deeply resonated with countless different folks.

On the surface, it's such a simple notion. It's a bumper sticker! But people across the country didn't treat it like anything so prosaic.

I considered its appeal, long and hard, and came to a basic realization. When people listened, they were responding to something that corresponded with the very depths of their soul. The song is a call to that "place" within us that doesn't want to hold grudges, doesn't want to harbor resentments, doesn't want to keep score of who's upping whom in the latest battle within an ongoing war that often seems never to wind down.

We love "Don't Worry, Be Happy" because it *does* seem to come from our heart.

Deep inside each of us is what I like to think of as the Cabana Place. A place where the sun is shining, a gentle, cooling breeze is blowing, and we, mai tai in hand, are settled into the most comfortable lounge chair on the cleanest, most beautiful beach.

We haven't a care in the world.

We're *relaxed*. Finally, fully, and truly, we are relaxed.

No hard feelings. No nagging bitterness. Nobody's fighting or upsetting or affronting us.

There, we've abandoned our anger. We've lost it. It can't find us.

Wouldn't it be great if we could be in the Cabana Place all the time—or at least anytime we wanted to be?

Well, guess what? We can.

If you want to transport yourself, almost anytime you wish, into your Cabana Place, merely think of someone who angers you—and forgive him.

Release your issues with him. Anything you hold against him, drop like a heavy suitcase you're no longer willing to carry.

Just like that, you'll feel yourself relaxing. You'll unwind. Your concerns will roll off you like water off the back of a Caribbean duck.

Want to be happy and not worry? *Forgive.*

Empowering others through not judging them

When you live a life primarily defined by your capacity and readiness to forgive others under conditions and in situations nobody would expect you to, you discover that you begin to change in ways you barely could've imagined before you started living in that fashion.

Living as one who readily forgives has changed my life. I mean, literally.

A lot of people work for me. Without them, New Life wouldn't work at all. I think everybody there is proud of what we do, and everyone who's part of it wants New Life to do its work better, more efficiently, and for more and more people. All the people on our team have made it their life's business, in one way or another, to reach out to broken souls and help them come to the only source that ultimately heals any of us: the flowing, cleansing waters of Jesus Christ's love.

That's what we do. That's what we are. And if I can say so, one of the big reasons we function so effectively is that I made a habit, long ago, of *empowering people through simply and consistently not judging them.*

If you judge someone, what you're saying is that you are so far above him that it's not only natural but also right for you to determine, in an absolute sense, the value of what he does and says and believes. The value of *him.*

If I, as head of New Life, go around my office pronouncing judgments on, over, and about those who work here, I know what will happen, what the effects will be. My staff will lock down on me like oysters closing their shells. They'll cease relating to me. They'll quit engaging me. Sensing that I'll judge them harshly, they'll stop being honest with me. Instead of the creative, productive back-and-forth on which I depend to make sure we keep arriving at the best, most helpful solutions possible, I'll be hearing "Yessir" and "Whatever you think, boss" and "Nice sweater, Steve!"

That would be my *first* clue something has gone terribly wrong. *Nobody* at New Life likes my sweaters. And they don't hide this very well. Though that's really a whole other concern. . . .

If you want people around you to become all they can, don't judge them. *Love* them.

Then step back, and watch them blossom.

And if you're ready for *your* life to blossom, please quit judging yourself harshly based on perfectionistic standards no one can achieve.

Don't worry so much. Be happy!

Questions for Discussion

1. What role do you think your anger plays in your life? Do you think others would agree with your perception of yourself in that regard?

2. Do you tend to judge people? Do you think your anger plays any role in how you assess them?

3. What was the angriest you got today? Why? How did you handle it?

4. What do you think about the relationship between the degree to which you're able to accept God's love for you and the degree to which your anger figures in your life?

5. In the rush of emotion, how do you tell or sense the difference between truly righteous anger and the kind of anger you'll later apologize for?

6. Do you think you ever use your anger as a means of avoiding anything you'd really rather not think about? What sorts of things might that be? Has using anger in that way proved good or helpful for you at all?

5

Give Up Instant Gratification;
Get Back Patience

(1) What Is Instant Gratification?

What's eating you?

One thing I've learned, from my (mumblety-mumble) years listening to *New Life Live* callers, is this: a massively corrosive facet of today's culture is the means by which anyone, nearly anytime, can have almost anything he wants to eat. If it's an hour before sunrise, and I want a turkey burger with an XL soda, I can get it. Craving a titanic chocolate sundae? Never a problem! Suddenly hankering for a sack of fried green tomatoes? Git 'er done.

Just about anything I want, at just about any moment I want it. Not much trouble getting it, either. *Probably don't even need the car. All-night market's close to the house. I could walk there.* That one-stop shop alone has enough goodies to keep me fat and sassy till I finally drop dead in their parking lot.

Impulse eating actually is an issue for me; I spend (seemingly, at least) half my life in hotels and airports. And I'm here to tell you, nobody is losing weight inside a hotel or an airport. Or if he is, he's exercising an amazing amount of willpower. Airports are filled with places and machines offering nearly every junk-food item in existence; hotels have plenty of the same, and many have 24-7 room service, where you merely push a button, speak your wish, and then try not to look like a total slob when the nice uniformed fellow shows up with the big tray on his squeaky-wheeled cart.

Munch, munch, munch.

Through New Life's *Lose It for Life* weekends, retreats, and events, I've interacted with thousands of people addicted to the instant gratification our eat-and-go culture proffers and pushes. When you're hungry and on the run, and you can pull right up to a window, stay in the car, order tasty stuff, and be back on the road within minutes, you're going to do it at least once.

Once you've done it once, it's easy to do it again.

Next thing you know, you haven't had a home-cooked meal in weeks.

Besides the awful things it does to your health, what does repeatedly succumbing to food-on-the-fly cost you? Significantly, the price includes one of your most important assets: *patience*.

When you can get anything you want whenever you want it, two things happen: your body stretches and your patience shrinks. There's no question we need to look at giving up instant gratification to get back patience.

Round-the-Clock Wired

It's already become one of those things people so often complain about that at this point we all feel we've heard it a million times. I'm afraid it's about to become one million and one.

What is the *deal* with drivers having one or both hands on their phones?

Believe it or not, I miss the days when *talking* on the phone was all anyone did behind the wheel. Then, they merely weaved across lanes, ignored lights and signs, and went either too fast or too slow. I could live with that; I even got to where I almost enjoyed, got an adrenaline rush from, the challenge of maneuvering around people trying to operate a vehicle while conversing. It gave my commute a sort of lively edge.

But now, with *texting* (and networking and Googling and playlisting) while driving? Road travel's almost a suicide/homicide run.

Okay, well, at least it's perilous enough that, like I say, I already miss the relatively recent "good ol' days." *Then,* you risked bumpers and quarter-panels. *Now,* as more and more drivers make driving their third priority, you nearly must consider whether that jaunt to the mall is worth risking your life.

Smartphones, smarter tablets, social networks, instant messaging, live conferencing . . . we live in the age of connectedness for sure. And much about it is wonderful. My wife and family can always reach me. I can stay in contact with friends and associates. The very short on-ramp to what we geriatrics still call "the information superhighway" is always a click away.

But you know what I think we're losing by being so readily and constantly accessible to so many people? By rarely (or never) stepping back from our "available" status, we're sacrificing being in touch with ourselves. If all I'm doing all the time is receiving and sending messages, ever being notified of and stimulated by yet another e-mail, call, text, or alert, then at the end of the day, I'm going to find that it will feel to me as if I haven't been alone with *me* the entire day.

Then, you know how else I'll feel? Impatient for another instant message.

When you can always get what you want

As I was thinking about what it means for any given person to at any moment pretty instantly secure for himself just about anything he wants, I thought of my friend David.

115

When David was young, he worked as a nanny (a manny?) for a married couple, the husband of which belonged to one of the world's three or four richest families. He often has told me about how strange it was to live in the home of people with limitless wealth.

I asked him if he'd be willing to write on what he thinks about the relationship between patience and always getting what you crave, *now*.

There was never any gap between [this couple's] experiencing of a desire, and that desire being met.

Like, let's say I wanted to learn how to play pool. Well, I might think about getting a table, if I was pretty rich—or I'd start looking around for nearby places where I could practice playing, et cetera.

That's not how this couple went about things at all. I used pool as an example, because one time the husband and I were walking around and, through a window, he saw some guys shooting pool.

"I want to play pool," he said.

So . . . we went home, and he got on the phone. And within two hours we had in the house a contractor, a crew, and two representatives from a company that sold pool tables.

Almost by the next day, one of his rooms had been transformed into a billiard room as nice as any you'd see anywhere. It was beautiful. They put gleaming hardwood paneling throughout the room; they built the wells and racks into the walls for the cues and supplies and all that stuff; they put in gorgeous new short-pile wall-to-wall carpeting; they hung a light over the table that appeared to be right out of the Roaring Twenties.

And the table! It looked like a museum piece. I think it cost $20,000; I can't imagine they would have paid anything less than that. When money's no object, you get the best. And you get whatever you want fast, too: the house was crawling with work people for one full day— and then they were gone. And suddenly we had the greatest pool room ever.

Within a week, the husband was bored with pool. He just quit going in that room. He was done.

That's how it was with everything with those two. Any desire, instantly met. And I'm not being mean when I say this, but they were the two unhappiest people you'd ever meet. They had no patience, whatsoever, for anything. Since their desires were never not met, their desires grew to control them. They needed constant stimulation.

I can't think of a better way to sum up how they both were than to say they had absolutely, 100 percent zero patience—ever.

That's the happiest I've ever been to come from a working-class background. Growing up, if we wanted something, we waited. We worked. We had patience. Not because we wanted to; reality *made* us.

Those people weren't living in reality. And because of their ability to get whatever they wanted whenever they wanted it, they had completely lost what I now think of as one of the greatest, most precious of the human virtues: patience.

(2) What Instant Gratification Does to Your Life

Creates impatience

What's fascinating about what David shared is how succinctly it captures the truth that instant gratification isn't born of impatience. Instead, *instant gratification creates impatience*. It's the cause of impatience.

We wouldn't necessarily think that. We tend to think a person constantly seeking instant gratification does so because she is, by nature, impatient.

I'm thinking of a woman, R., who's one of the most appetitive people I know. She's ever seeking, and securing, sensual gratification of one sort or another (most frequently food and drink). Whenever I'm around her and her husband, I always notice how impatient she is. And without really taking time to reflect on it, I sort of automatically attribute her intense passion for self-satisfaction to her being *naturally* impatient.

Once, R. ended up in the hospital. She was fine; it was routine surgery. (For the record, I really don't see how any surgery can be routine, if I'm the one facing the knife.) But it meant she had to stay overnight and then be at home, in bed, for a week.

When I went to visit, I was struck by how calm R. seemed. How relaxed.

How *patient*!

Then it hit me why R. seemed to have magically transformed into a veritable Gandhi: she *couldn't* be instantly gratified. She couldn't get out of bed! What she wanted, she had to delay.

About four days into it, R. had regained the patience I'd always just assumed she'd never had in the first place.

Approximately half a week. That's how long it took to restore her.

If you sense you might be overdriven toward instant gratification, take the R. test. For four days, give yourself only what you really need. Set aside anything you merely want.

See how you feel at the end of that time. Chances are, you'll feel more like the real you than you've felt in a very long time.

Creates dissatisfaction

As instant gratification creates impatience, it also spawns dissatisfaction. Which is odd, isn't it, when you consider that the whole idea of gratification is to be gratified. However, that's not the way gratification ultimately works.

At first, it is. Initially, when you acquire and dispose of that triple-decker bacon cheeseburger, you feel satisfied. "Hit the spot," you say.

That spot is, essentially, a *hole* the food filled.

Recently I was out with a business associate who, after dinner, produced an expensive cigar. While we continued our chat, he lit the thing and enjoyed it for the next half hour. The whole time he was puffing, he looked as contented as any man I'd ever seen. Relaxed;

nestled into a comfortable chair after a large, terrific meal; smiling like a cat who'd just nabbed the perfect canary.

"Ahh, that was ideal!" he happily declared, grinding out his butt. (Sorry. That's what he was doing.)

A week later, the same friend called me.

"Ever since the night with you I had that cigar," he said, "I've been craving another one! I never let myself smoke cigars; I love them so much that once I have one, I must have another.

"It's the craziest thing. I enjoy my cigars immensely, because they bring me so much satisfaction. But inevitably, the big byproduct is how *dissatisfied* it ends up making me feel. Now I feel like it's impossible for me to ever be happy again until I get another wonderful cigar.

"What's the matter with me, Steve? Am I crazy?"

I assured him that no, he isn't crazy. He's worse—he's human. Being an ex-smoker, I know just how human you can get when you combine something that goes in your mouth with the most addicting chemical I know of *and* an aroma only an aficionado appreciates. Very nearly irresistible.

Creates need for increased stimulus

It's common for people to insist that marijuana isn't a "gateway" drug; that indulging in it doesn't give rise to desire for more powerful psychotropic hallucinogens or stimulants.

I enjoy working in the field of mental and spiritual health. One thing I like most is reading and learning about all the theories proffered by fellow professionals. Almost always, I find their discoveries in agreement with my own experience. People tend to be pretty much the same, no matter who they are, where they come from, or what their individual psychological challenge. I rarely hear or read of a study or finding in the realm of Christian counseling that doesn't resonate with me as elementally reasonable and true.

119

Nonetheless, no matter how many times I hear marijuana isn't a gateway drug—and no matter how many degrees are on the wall of the person or persons saying it—I always disagree. I might not stand up at a conference of my associates and howl, "*Balderdash!*" But I'll sure be thinking something along those lines.

I don't think I've ever known a young person who began smoking weed who didn't sooner or later end up involved with heavier drugs. Now, I also don't know all that many young people who smoke pot; that crowd and mine don't mix much. But they do mix enough and *have* mixed enough for me to say with confidence that once a person (especially an impressionable youth, and what such person isn't impressionable?) starts on pot, he starts seeking stronger and stronger stimuli.

To be blunt, pretending this doesn't happen is plain silly.

"Some" of just about anything that feels good tends to make you want more of that thing.

Only just a little stronger. A little bigger. A little longer-lasting. A bit more.

You've boarded a train that's moving forward, one from which a tragic number of people, years later, find themselves incapable of disembarking.

Caters to the worst side of you

There isn't a single way in which ongoing instant gratification benefits your character. It doesn't make you nobler, more honorable, gentler, more loving, more patient, or more helpful to others. It doesn't make you more conscientious. It doesn't make you neater or cleaner. It doesn't make you kinder to animals. It doesn't give you a longer attention span.

It doesn't do *anything* but make you a more miserable person on the inside, one whom fewer and fewer others, on the outside, want to be with. Every effect of habitual instant gratification is negative.

There's no upside to being one who's made it his constant business to be perpetually sated.

> Stay alert! Watch out for your great enemy, the devil. He prowls around like a roaring lion, looking for someone to devour.
>
> —1 Peter 5:8

That, in a nutshell, is the whole dynamic. That's how an unbridled drive toward excessive self-pleasing feels: malevolence prowling around like a predator. In this context, the lion is *you,* on the hunt for more and more of whatever sensual thing has caught you in the grips of its stimulation.

If you feel your drives toward instant gratification have become that beast, tame yourself. Put that part of you back into the cage where it belongs.

And don't let it back out! Desires for satisfaction that initially can seem harmless as a kitten soon enough turn into a ravenous creature you couldn't wrestle to the ground if you'd been eating Wheaties for a month.

> Don't you realize that your body is the temple of the Holy Spirit, who lives in you and was given to you by God? You do not belong to yourself, for God bought you with a high price. So you must honor God with your body.
>
> —1 Corinthians 6:19–20

Let your lion lie down with the Lamb.

(3) How to Give Up Instant Gratification

Try it for a week/day/minute

Solomon was just a wee little man when he was drawn to the water in our backyard. When he was a few months old, we all got into the pool for our Christmas picture; he fell asleep in my arms before the photo could be snapped. One of my favorite images is of me kissing that boy as he rests in my arms in the warm water.

When he grew to age two, we started to have a lot of water fun. I'd hold him, spin him around, and do piggyback rides all over that pool. He loved it.

He would stand on the side, then jump in, sink down, and come up smiling. He had no fear of the water, which was one reason we had to thoroughly babyproof outdoors.

Solomon also began to make major life-decisions. Eat or not eat. Sleep or cause Mom and Dad hours of irritation. And go in the water or not. But *that* was always a go—probably because I never eased him into the pool like it was something to fear.

It was sink or swim. Do or don't. No tiptoeing. There was no in-between.

In regard to instant gratification, I think this is similar to how we're wired. If you'd like to try your hand at backing away from the habits that have you trapped—don't. Instead, *run* away. Dive completely into *not* doing whatever thing it is you feel essentially helpless to stop doing.

Realize the fleeting nature of "the quick input"

The part about instant gratification that we sometimes fail to take seriously enough is the *instant* part. Gratification itself is good.

It's common for someone to come up to me, after a three-day New Life intensive workshop, and say the event changed her life. A man will say he can tell—honestly, truly know—that the grip pornography's had on him is gone. A woman, with tears in her eyes, will say she finally understands why, ever since she can remember, she's been addicted to food. Or someone will call our broadcast show and share that the advice we gave a year ago has worked so well that he's back and delighted in marriage with his once-estranged wife.

When this happens, I feel *gratified*. It makes me feel great to know we're changing lives. (Meaning, at New Life we're helping people to help *Jesus* change their lives. It's always God.)

When I run a 5K or 10K (or the one marathon I completed), I experience gratification if, over the course of the race, I've somehow managed to resist doing what I always want to do, which is, halfway through, pretending that in my encroaching senility I got lost, unintentionally veered off the course, and happened to turn up at a pizza pub. If (yet again!) I didn't, but instead actually finished without publicly embarrassing myself, then, yes, I'm gratified.

Feeling gratified is *good*.

Feeling *instantly* gratified? That's a whole other can of not-so-good.

Instant gratification doesn't require any work. It doesn't take any discipline. Nobody trains to get it. There's no process to being instantly gratified—beyond, say, grab/bite/chew/swallow/repeat.

That's why *nobody really enjoys instant gratification*. If you're stuck in its cycle, the only thing you have is momentary pleasure. There's nothing very real about such "enjoyment." It has no substance. It's like a magic trick: seems that something wonderful and fantastic is happening . . . but it's not.

You're not honestly having any fun at all.

That's why in the end I cross the finish line. I know exactly what would happen if I did abandon the pursuit. I'd be inhaling my pizza, gulping my soda—and staring out the window, wishing I'd stayed in the race.

The true cost of quick satisfaction

Another thing about instant gratification: it doesn't seem to involve very much. It happens quickly and often isn't expensive. Everywhere you go, for instance, you're invited to stop for a moment, spend a buck or a few, and walk off with food that might have a certain greasy appeal but will be so health-detrimental that you may as well have eaten a deep-fried stick of butter.

It didn't cost you a lot of time or money. You got your quick fix and kept on moving.

It's partly due to the hyper-transitory nature of the instant-gratification experience that we rarely consider the full cost of the toll we paid to zip down that road. It's hard to invest time considering the real impact on your life occasioned by that McDonald's bag, sitting next to you on the console, when all you're thinking about is not being late for the meeting that's about to start.

You bought that junk food effortlessly. It took relatively little money. It all happened so rapidly.

What you don't grasp is that, in reality, you paid for it with one of your most precious possessions.

You purchased it with your dignity.

Not all of it. I'm not suggesting that a prince who buys a double-pounder with quadruple cheese at Fatty's to Go-Go leaves a bum.

But when you walked out of that joint, you did leave behind part of something priceless. How many times can you make that transaction before there's a real, big, noticeable chunk of your self-worth missing?

You can't afford to keep paying that premium. No one can.

Nobody but you necessarily knows when you've compromised your dignity through instant gratification. You can act like that family-size bag of chips meant nothing. You can pretend that porno movie wasn't so big a deal. You can tell yourself one little sneaky cigarette doesn't add up to much.

Deep down, though, you know that isn't true.

You're still cognizant of what you did. And you realize that the beast of instant gratification has no interest in tempting you toward onetime exceptions. It wants to own you, to control every choice, to keep being fed.

You're aware that you're purposefully, willfully, methodically selling yourself short.

You're not honoring yourself.

You're trading dignity for a fast fill and a fleeting feeling.

"Only a few dollars," here and there, actually isn't quite the bargain you thought you were getting.

(4) Gaining Back Patience

Reflecting upon God's permanence

Lately I've been reading an enthralling document I discovered online. It's a diary, from 1865, transcribed from the original found in the attic of an Iowa farmhouse. It was written by a mother as she and her family made slow progress westward in a wagon train across the Great Plains.

What I find so compelling is the diary's tone. It's clear that, even though the woman and her family are going through hardships the likes of which I can barely imagine, none of what she endures particularly bothers or upsets her. She never loses her calm, her confidence, her hope, her appreciation for the beauty of the land all around her.

She has a job to do. She's doing it.

She's aware of the work it entails. And she's plainly attuned to the dangers: she has five children who, as the train plods along, forever are running wild in this very wild region (rather than indoors or in a backyard).

Five children. On that journey!

If I simultaneously get all my kids into the van and get us safely to the grocery store, I almost feel like I've managed and navigated a harrowing, cross-country adventure. Well, I might have felt something like that, until I read this diary. Talk about having your own daily life put into perspective.

The more I read of this woman's writing, the more I began to understand why she was almost divinely serene. She *believed* in God.

It's not so much that she believed moving the family across tremendous distance was God's calling. If that was part of her motivation, she doesn't indicate it. What she does convey is that throughout the trip she never for a moment doubted that God was with them, on every step across every acre. She seemed particularly aware that God was in the *land* around her.

That, I finally realized, was what so clearly kept her in such a state of grace. Everywhere she looked—at the vast plains, at the verdant grass, at the blooming trees, at the flowing rivers, at the golden hills—she saw God.

She saw God's work. She saw God's majesty.

She knew she was in God's country. Knowing this instilled in her a profound patience.

You are in God's country, too. We all are.

There's no good reason we should be any less patient.

Availing yourself of the richer pleasures of knowing God

As just about any therapist knows, one of the most important things you can do for a person struggling to give up an addiction is teach him to substitute something else for what he's addicted to. If he doesn't then learn to substitute something good, he'll substitute something not good.

For example, if you give up whiskey and don't start to recover, you pick up a body instead of a bottle and sexual addiction becomes a driving force. It's a pretty straightforward stratagem. If someone's addicted to nicotine, behavioral modification techniques can be employed such that eventually the desire for, say, a lollipop can replace the yearning for a smoke.

Years and years ago, I had a friend, Tom, who underwent exactly this treatment: he became trained to associate his cravings for cigarettes with suckers that have candy in the middle. I had recommended his therapist.

One evening Tom phoned.

"Steve," he said, "you've got to help me."

"Of course. What's the problem?"

"Problem is, I'm now thoroughly addicted to suckers. I'm eating about thirty of those dumb things a day."

"Oh. Gosh. That doesn't sound very good."

"No. It's *not!* It's not good at all. I have suckers in my jacket pockets. In my car. In my desk. On my nightstand! It's *ridiculous.*

"The good news is, I don't smoke anymore. The bad news is, pretty soon I'm going to have to get *dentures,* because all my *teeth* will have fallen out. I blame you for this, Steve. Help me!"

(I did; he's fine.)

If you are constantly seeking immediate gratification, *consider*—ideally, whenever you get the urge to quickly gratify whatever habitual craving is keeping you from the patience you know you need—*availing yourself of the much, much richer pleasures of knowing God.*

It's true enough that candy isn't a great improvement over Camels. Taking a moment, though, just before you take a step in a negative direction—for example, just before you take the next bite for which you're not actually hungry—to stop and think about God? *That's* an improvement.

If you do this for just a little while, soon you'll find yourself in the position, almost without even noticing, of having substituted for something that at best gave brief pleasure (and at worst was hastening your premature demise) something that, no matter how you look at it, *cannot* be bested.

Don't reach for those websites or for that pint of ice cream. *Reach for God.*

If you are to stop the cycle, you also need to reach for a fellow struggler.

I serve as teaching pastor at Heartland Church in Indianapolis. I asked two fellow pastors to go to lunch with me and told them about my struggles following a couple of surgeries. I was exercising less; once I got out of my routine, it wasn't so easy to resume. Along

127

with this came extra snacking as I coped with the pain of recovery. I was ten pounds heavier than I wanted to be.

They said they wanted to lose some weight also. Then, their first question was, "Steve, if someone called your show and presented the same situation, what would you suggest?"

I answered, "This."

"This?"

"Yes, this. I'd tell them to find a couple of buddies who'd encourage one another and hold each other accountable."

And that's what we did as we started our trek to lose two pounds a week.

Instantly the battle was easier. I'd replaced my problem with connection, support, and accountability; it made all the difference in the world.

So my question for you is, "What needs replacing in your life?"

And then, "What wonderful thing could you replace it with?"

Go ahead and get started!

Making God's love enough

There's a sense in which we humans are a pretty complicated group.

Each person is a phenomenon. We have so many dimensions to who we are and how we are and why we do the things we do in exactly the way we do them. At any given moment there's so infinitely much going on with any given person that . . . well, for one, it's a mystery to me how anybody, in light of how indecipherable they *themselves* are, can arrive at the conclusion that there's no God.

As definitionally difficult to pin down as people are, though, we do, all of us, have some commonalities. One is that, generally speaking, we want more.

We've looked at this already: we get some of something—and if that something hits us just the right way, then we want more of the same.

If some is good, more must be better. That driving paradigm is basically hardwired into our existence.

128

A worthwhile thing to think about is whether or not there might be any inherently common thread in our apparently disparate cravings. If Joe constantly turns to overeating, and Janet can't stop smoking, and Paul cannot stay away from X-rated stuff, is there anything each compulsion—that all such desires and responses, had and done by anyone—truly has in common?

Is there a unifying reality to all drives toward instant gratification? Is there any sense in which *all* those things could, in fact, be *one* thing?

I think there is. I think anyone and everyone who's fallen victim to habitual instant gratification actually, really is after God's love.

Without God's love, a hole exists. All the donuts, drinks, and porn in the world can't fill it.

If God's love isn't enough, then you can trust that nothing will ever be.

About this dynamic, think, if you would, on Romans 8:38–39:

> I am convinced that nothing can ever separate us from God's love. Neither death nor life, neither angels nor demons, neither our fears for today nor our worries about tomorrow—not even the powers of hell can separate us from God's love. No power in the sky above or in the earth below—indeed, nothing in all creation will ever be able to separate us from the love of God that is revealed in Christ Jesus our Lord.

In other words, you already have everything you could possibly desire. Flush those french fries. Connect with God through prayer. Pick up the phone and talk with someone. Soon you'll discover: you're already full.

(5) Living a Life Filled With Patience

The return (and pleasure) of the disciplined life

It's a shame so many of us today have so many frown-faced associations with the word *discipline*.

Not too long ago I attended a local school board meeting. One topic that came up for discussion was how best to deal with the problem of truancy.

The man sitting next to me stood up and said, "What's most important to do with these school kids is to remember that there is nothing like good old-fashioned discipline to—"

And what a ruckus rose up to interrupt! You'd have thought he'd demanded that the district establish a torture policy for children late to class.

I guess everyone *thought* he was going to say that kids these days need a dose of corporal punishment. They shouted him down before he could finish.

Later he told me:

All I was going to say was that we should teach kids the joys of living a disciplined life. I wasn't going to say to *beat* kids. I was going to say that it's good for kids to live a disciplined life, that children like order, and routine, and knowing that if they simply do certain things, every single day, then they surely will get the results that *they* want. Discipline grounds the life of a child. It gives them purpose, patience—a sense of process, rather than what we have today, which is kids being everywhere encouraged to think that they can instantly have just about anything they want. But, boy! You even raise the question of discipline as it relates to children any more, and you better watch out!

He's right. Living a disciplined life, far from being onerous or damaging, is one of the most *rewarding* things anyone can do.

The simple, liberating fact is, if you want to reclaim the patience that instant gratification so utterly destroys, assume a disciplined life in God. As Paul puts it:

Those who are dominated by the sinful nature think about sinful things, but those who are controlled by the Holy Spirit think about things that please the Spirit. So letting your sinful nature control your mind leads to death. But letting the Spirit control your mind leads to life and peace. For the sinful nature is always hostile to God. It never did obey God's laws, and it never will. That's why those who are still under the control of their sinful nature can never please God.

But you are not controlled by your sinful nature. You are controlled by the Spirit if you have the Spirit of God living in you.

—Romans 8:5–9

A more generous attitude toward others

At a *Lose It for Life* weekend, "Suzy" was delivered of her obsession with food. Because of some things she later told me about how that weekend also impacted her relationships with others, I contacted her to ask if she'd write briefly on that subject.

Below is part of Suzy's generous response.

I had the realization that I was substituting food for the love of God, [and] everything changed for me. And I would say that one of the biggest changes—one I wouldn't have expected in a million years— was that I found I grew a lot more patient with others than I've ever felt before. To be honest, before the change, I wasn't actually aware I *was* impatient with people. I always thought I was just . . . normal in that regard.

I [realized, though,] that nobody I dealt with (and I don't mean my family, whom of course I love with all my heart, but people I work with, or simply interact with as I'm going about my everyday business) ever seemed to ever be quite smart enough or careful enough or caring enough—or *good* enough, somehow, is what it really all boiled down to.

I'm so ashamed to admit I used to feel that way about people— and, much worse, used to *act* as if I felt that way. But I really did! . . .

All that harsh negativity disappeared once I was full of the love of the King of Kings, instead of full of (as, God knows, was usual with me) the food of Burger King. I found I simply had a lot more patience with people. I think that's because, knowing for the first time that Jesus really *did* forgive me (being raised a Christian, I'd known that all my life; I'd just never *known* known it!), I naturally felt a lot more forgiving of others. I was more *generous* with them.

Where before I know I would have felt impatient or irritated or annoyed by someone maybe being slower than I thought they should be, or maybe not getting some stupid thing or other just the way I thought it should be, now I've felt patient, generous, loving!

Now that I'm living with the love of Jesus in my heart, I don't know how I ever lived without it. And I definitely don't know how anyone ever lived with me.

Tell your listeners and readers that if they want to know what it means to be generous and patient with others, *all the time,* there's only one thing to do: stop feeding sensual "needs" with foods and all the other stuff we don't need, and instead start feeding the heart with the only thing anyone really needs at all, the love of the Lord.

Consider yourself told.

Trusting God's time

When we're impatient, what we're really saying is that we know better than God.

"I want this thing to be *this* way, right now," or "I want this guy to do and be what I want him to do and be—*right now*" is exactly the same as saying, "God doesn't know what he's doing."

Imagine ever actually saying that to God. You wouldn't dare! But that's what you *are* saying whenever you needlessly take the attitude of impatience.

Say you're a mechanic, working on a car. You've gone pretty deeply into the engine; parts and tools and components are everywhere around. The whole thing is up on a lift.

You hear a man holler, "Hey! Send out my car!"

You emerge from beneath the passenger door. "Excuse me?"

"My car!" he says, impatiently. "That's my car. I want to drive it now."

"You can't. I mean . . . look at it. Clearly not road-ready, right?"

"I don't care if it's *ready*! It's mine, and I want to drive it somewhere!"

"But I'm fixing it. It's not finished. You brought it in this morning for a two-day repair."

"I don't care what kind of deal we had. This is now. And I want my car!"

Wouldn't you think you're dealing with a crazy person? Wouldn't you wonder how he could possibly be so unreasonable?

And yet you demand that God make things the way you want them to be, right when you want them to be that way.

Meanwhile, he's working on the world, making it, in his time, just the way he knows it should be.

Once you surrender to God your need to always have everything you want, you'll see that what you *thought* you wanted cannot possibly compare to the greatness and perfection of what God has in store for you, me, and everyone else who believes in and puts their faith on his divine providence.

All you need to have a truly fulfilling, truly peaceful life is to trust in God. You must believe that God, ultimately, is in control of everything that ever has happened, is happening, or will happen, and that all of it, no matter how difficult or harmful it might seem, will, in the end, resound to his glory.

You can be impatient; you can demand exactly what you want, exactly when you want it; you can insist that your car is ready to drive, even when the only person in a position to fix it is telling you it's not.

You can keep yourself in that sort of ongoing agitation. Or you can let the Master Mechanic do his job, and then call you when it's time.

Questions for Discussion

1. Do you feel you're addicted to anything? If so, how has that addiction affected your life?

2. What efforts do you make to unplug yourself from media? How often do you do so? If you do unplug, how does it make you feel? Restless? Relaxed? And how does it feel to go back to it?

3. If you're doing a lot of overindulging, what finally reins you back in?

4. In what area of your life do you feel you're the most disciplined? Why that area, do you think?

5. Can you think of an example where you got frustrated that things weren't going the way you wanted, only to realize later that they had gone much better than in any way you could have anticipated?

6

Give Up Learned Helplessness;
Get Back Power

(1) What Is Learned Helplessness?

Feeling unempowered

There's nothing worse than feeling that, when it comes to anything you care about, there's nothing you can do. We all know this feeling; it's prone to come over most of us when we open the newspaper or watch a little news.

All those starving children in Africa we're unable to feed. War in the Middle East we're helpless to stop. Crime happening everywhere, and we can't do a preventative thing. A whole family got caught up in a flashflood.

Just goes on and on and on, doesn't it? With the twenty-four-hour news cycle immersing us, and with all the news that negative, it's a wonder any of us ever can scrape up any sense of power and influence at all. Anywhere we look, it seems, we come into contact with

135

another dreadful occurrence or action that we personally can't do much of anything to affect.

For a lot of us, that really hurts. After being exposed to myriad examples of the disparity between what's *happening* in the world and what we're in a position to *do* about it, we can start feeling like we want to just crawl into our own little lives, insulate ourselves, turn to self-comfort, and stop trying to engage. We feel depressed, stressed, afraid.

But just as daunting as the world-at-large can seem if experienced through a certain kind of lens (especially if that lens is on a TV camera), so our everyday lives can seem daunting if seen through the lens of learned helplessness. Consider how many times a day you say to yourself things like:

> I can't do that.
> I can't fix that.
> I can't have that.
> I can't win that.
> I can't achieve that.
> I can't say that.
> I can't handle that.
> I can't be that.

I can't; I can't; I can't.

Sometimes, of course, it's true: sometimes you *can't* have, do, be, fix, attain, or win whatever "it" is. You can want to flap your arms and fly with every ounce of desire in your heart, but your actual relationship with gravity won't change. You may think how much fun it would be to become invisible whenever you wish, but alas, you're stuck in a material body that anyone can see—or will see, as soon as you or someone else turns on the light.

How you might feel about not being able to fly on demand or become volitionally invisible isn't the kind of helplessness I want to discuss here. *Anyone* would feel helpless in those scenarios. Those are objective, universal "shortcomings"; they're not subjective and personal.

I'm not interested in the challenges you can't overcome for the simple reason that no one can.

I'm interested in the challenges you *can* meet and beat but *think* you can't, because somewhere along the line of your life (and probably back near the start) you bought into the lie that you're a whole lot weaker than you are.

In more ways than you think, I know you *can* fly. And it's time for you to know it, too.

Feeling hopeless

It's been my experience that, overall, there are two kinds of people on earth: those who feel empowered to do and be whatever they choose, and those who feel like whatever is, *is,* and that there's not much they or anyone else can do about it.

Guess which type tends to be a lot happier?

Feeling like you can't do much to impact the quality or dynamics of your own life is like being trapped in a body-sized drawer. You sense you're locked into your current state. You're dependent upon conditions outside your input for everything you really need just to survive, much less thrive. You stay in place; you can't do much. Your options are extremely limited. Your view never changes. You go nowhere.

And what do confined people tend to *do?* Sit a lot, that's what. What else is there? When you're helpless to change anything about the way you're living, or most if not all the conditions that define your everyday experience, what soon settles over you is a sense of profound, unalleviated boredom.

Prisoners may be angry and restless, and interested in figuring out when the laundry truck arrives so at the right moment they can jump in and escape. Mostly, though, they're *bored.* So they sit. They lie down. And they give up. They get defeated by the unchangeable conditions of their environment. At best, many of them wait for a better day to come.

When you really are helpless, too, you learn not to have any hope at all—not for being entertained, not for being encouraged, not for producing anything of value. You stop participating. You stop caring. You shut down.

You sit. You lie down. You give up.

Well, if you do feel that way about yourself and your life, then you are in a jail. A penitentiary of your learned helplessness. That kind of prison is every bit as oppressive and depressing as any actual dungeon. And it can be just as hard to escape from, also.

Nevertheless, know this: we *can* break you free from whatever confinement you've constructed for yourself out of the bricks and bars someone else contributed, and for which someone else drew up blueprints.

You might feel you literally are locked inside an unbreachable cell. But you aren't. You just haven't found the right keys.

Let's find them.

Accepting false limitations

I know a woman, "Lilly," who was raised poor. And I mean *poor* poor. When she was a little girl, she used to eat snow on her long hikes to school, to stave off raging hunger. She would mix dirt in with the snowballs, too, just so there would be a little substance in her breakfast.

Lilly's father was the town drunk. Whatever little money her mother could scrape together off their tiny, meager farm, or by selling the doilies she furiously knit in hopes anybody would want one, her father drank away.

I'll spare you all other sorts of details about the hardships Lilly suffered, but trust me: she was as poor as people can be. Her whole

138

life was about when and what she was going to eat and then how she could stay warm at night.

With a bare amount of education, Lilly left home when she was fifteen.

I knew that if I stayed in that town, my life would be one big fat nothing. I saw it everywhere around me: poor people who understood their lives as mainly just one long experience in suffering and boredom until the good Lord saw fit to call them home. That was it.

Not only did most of the people not really have lives, they didn't really expect to. Poverty does that; it robs you of your hope. You know nothing's ever going to change, so you give up hoping it might. You just . . . resolve yourself to having more in common with a donkey than you do anyone who, say, lives in a city and has a good job. You don't even think about stuff like that for yourself. All you worry about is whether or not you have enough money to meet your basic needs.

So I got out. I looked older than I was; I moved two hundred miles to the biggest city nearest us, and the moment I got off the bus, I swore to myself that I wouldn't do one other thing before I got myself a job. I wouldn't eat; I wouldn't worry about where I was going to sleep that night; I wouldn't worry about storing my bag anywhere—nothing. I would walk out of that bus station, onto a busy street, and I would start going into office buildings and businesses, telling my story, and asking for work.

I could barely read; I had no training beyond simple farm labor; I knew nothing about the world. I'd never seen buildings as big as the first ones I saw when I stepped off that bus. But I knew that I needed a job, and I knew I couldn't do a single thing until I got one. So that's what I decided to get—right there, that day. As long as I had a mouth, and could talk, I was getting myself a *job* that day.

Today, Lilly is a *very* successful businesswoman. She owns a huge real estate management company, and that's just one business of hers.

The world told Lilly she couldn't. She wasn't educated enough. She wasn't prepared enough. She wasn't even *old* enough.

Lilly ignored all that, and she did it anyway. She didn't accept the limitations on her life that, in her heart of hearts, she knew were false.

If an uneducated, impoverished, inexperienced teenager can do what she did, can anything in the world stop you from making your life a success?

(2) What Learned Helplessness Does to Your Life

Ruins chances of personal evolution

There's no question about it, "Judy" was pretty. The kind of pretty that makes store employees and restaurant staff overlook what they're supposed to be doing; makes delivery guys just hand over the pizza and forget about getting paid; makes mechanics throw in an engine overhaul on top of a simple oil change. I can honestly say I used to be uncomfortable walking across busy intersections with Judy; I'd be glancing in four different directions, just waiting for the inevitable nine-car, distracted-driver pileup.

Judy's looks were a blessing to her—but as I came to discover, they also were a curse. Everything had always come easy. Attractiveness had allowed her to glide through life, never having to do much to get the kinds of things other people have to work for. Although it wasn't quite this bad, it *was* almost as if Judy only had to stand there, and everything a person could want would land at her feet.

Cars. House. Jewelry. Career. Plus, did I mention she was an extremely well-paid fashion model? (Did I *have* to?)

Further, it wasn't like she had to cheapen herself to get such things. And she didn't.

What Judy did do, around age thirty, was marry a man so wealthy the U.S. Treasury must have been direct-shipping him half their freshly pressed bills.

About ten years later, Judy needed help. Her problem was, she'd never learned to personally evolve. She had no sense of individual empowerment, of being able to actively engage in the kinds of things most people do whenever they want to move from wherever they are to a place or station that's better.

Since everyone had always done everything for her, she didn't know how to do anything for herself. That may sound like a "boo-hoo, something spilled on the calf-leather seat of my million-dollar Bentley" problem, but it isn't.

Now in her forties, Judy wanted her own life. The husband she'd divorced had turned out to be a mean-spirited creep. Out on her own, she sought to make her way in the world doing something real and credible, something not predicated on her being otherworldly beautiful.

"I feel so *stupid*," she literally cried out. "I can't do *anything*. I want a life. I want to build something I can be proud of. Yet I feel so helpless."

So we got to work on empowering Judy to see past her learned helplessness toward a future that she built for herself.

Well, not entirely by herself. The very Sunday following the first time Judy came to me seeking to get past helplessness, she began attending church.

Finally, in Jesus, someone in her corner cared about her soul and not merely her looks. She also started attending a home group—she didn't just show up at church but also became involved, an active part of its community.

Ruins chances of professional progress

"Steve," said Don, one of the managers who worked with me. "We've got a problem with Carl."

"What is it?" (Carl was a truly good guy. I liked him and was distressed to hear there might be anything wrong with his work.)

"I don't know—that's what I want your help with. As I think you know, I've had a lot of hope in Carl. He's bright; has a great attitude; works hard."

"Promote him!" I said. "Problem solved."

Don laughed. "I wish. Actually, that's something I figured I *would* be doing sooner or later. In the last couple months, though, I've seen Carl kind of . . . I don't know how to say it . . . bump up against some sort of wall. Since he started here, I've been giving him more and more responsibilities, and he's done just fine with them. Until lately. He's begun to . . . well, fail."

"That's not good."

"No, it's not. The thing is, I can't figure out *why*. It seems, suddenly, that he's making one mistake after another. And I can tell the tasks aren't anything he can't grasp; I know he can do the things where he's coming up short. That's what's so weird. I can't understand it."

"Drugs, maybe? Drinking?"

"No. I mean, I don't think so. I know how to spot those signs; I see none of them with Carl. Can you talk to him, Steve? See if you can help get him back on track?"

So I did. And we got Carl back on track.

Know what his problem turned out to be? *He thought he was dumb.*

Carl thought that in our company he'd gone as far as "someone of his capacity" would allow. So assuming he was too limited to properly handle the new responsibilities he'd been given, he failed at them.

I'd been talking with him regularly for about two weeks when I seized upon the true nature of his issue: from a very young age, his father had trained him to think of himself as stupid.

That was why Carl was failing. That was his mental block. That was the knot inside him that needed untying.

We untied it.

Guess who went on to become one of the best assets *anyone's* ever had?

Learned helplessness had been ruining Carl's chance to personally—and professionally—evolve. If you're finding your own progress being stymied, remember: among the surest ways to get a vehicle moving forward is to take your foot off the brake.

The road awaits!

Never holding the reins of your own buggy

Do you know someone who always seems to be in the midst of a personal storm? Her cell phone never stops ringing, she keeps missing appointments, she has parties and events (to be thrown and attended) ad infinitum, she's never on time for a meeting . . . she has, in general, fires burning wildly all over the place.

She never seems to be paying real attention to you, or anything you might be saying. She doesn't even seem to be paying attention to herself—to what she's doing and saying. Everything around her has the aura of turmoil.

What's really happening with people who are "living" this way?

Often what it *seems* like is that they're very, very busy—even very productive. They're out in the world; they know lots and lots of folks.

It's obvious that they're constantly in the middle of more things than they can keep track of or handle. In every way, they seem almost frantically and frightfully "involved" with life.

However (and this inevitably becomes clear once you really get to know someone stuck on that thrill ride), they're not really *involved* with—vested in, filled with, committed to—life at all. They're not truly engaging, connecting with the innumerable people and happenings surrounding them. They're pacing themselves at a sprint so they don't have to deal with the reality that, when the text messages stop coming, they feel desperately out of control.

They feel helpless.

At the other end of the spectrum are people who seemingly won't involve themselves in anything. They rarely go anywhere; they don't open themselves up to new experiences; they never follow their curiosity to unfamiliar places and thoughts. Instead of embracing life, they sit on its sidelines and let it pass right by. Whereas the "overactive" person often seems to have a gregarious personality, these folks appear mainly morose and listless.

They, as much as the fully wired socialites, have become captives of learned helplessness. They likewise feel powerless.

When you've been defeated by learned helplessness, what you feel—no matter how those feelings actually manifest in your personality—is that you are life's victim. Everyone else, and everything else, has the power; you can only react to what's already happened and already been decided. You can't be proactive; you can't get behind the wheel of your own car and drive.

You're always being towed somewhere. Essentially, along for the ride.

(3) How to Give Up Learned Helplessness

Watch yourself

One thing I've definitely learned while counseling people on how to get past what's inhibiting them from allowing themselves to be fully healed (by Jesus, of course—no other power can perform such a miracle): simple and clearheaded observation is among the most powerful tools any of us has for really understanding what's going on within oneself.

"The unexamined life is not worth living," wrote Plato. And while he may have meant that more philosophically or abstractly, I understand the value of his enjoinment very practically. Again, one of the most effective, easy-to-use therapeutic tools available to anyone seeking freedom from a psychological or spiritual problem is to observe the mind. To simply, straightforwardly examine life—from the inside.

I often suggest that a person step back from his mind, just a bit, and spend one whole day essentially tracking what he thinks and feels. If he has a problem with anger, I recommend (as I did earlier) that for a day he watches what triggers it. If he has an issue with frequent anxiety, I ask him to go about his life but, throughout the course of one day, mark when he finds himself feeling anxious. In this way, patterns of conditions and responses can begin to emerge, which can allow us to bring something that on the whole seems broad, unwieldy, and even unmanageable under the control we need to begin working toward a real and lasting solution.

If you feel helpless, instead of trying to outright eradicate that feeling, spend a day noticing what brings it up. Live like you would on any other day, but carry at all times a pad and pen. When you find yourself feeling helpless, mark the time and the situation you were in when you realized the feeling.

Whom were you talking with? What was happening? How long did the feeling last? What did it resolve itself into—what feeling, in other words, eventually replaced it?

At the end of that day—or perhaps the next, after a good night's sleep—look at your list. Carefully go over each of the entries.

Pick one. Put yourself back in the moment it records. Start to relive that experience. And then, in the middle of that replay, freeze it. Just hold yourself right there.

Step back from yourself—from the you who's frozen in that moment. Observe yourself standing there, with everything and everyone exactly as it was when the feeling of helplessness came over you.

What happened, exactly? Who or what was making you feel helpless?

Were you *truly* helpless? Or just imagining that you were?

If you were imagining that you were helpless when, in fact, you weren't, the question is: why?

Why, right then, did your "default feeling" go to helplessness?

Where did you learn to do that?

Who taught it to you?

Whom in your past are you serving by giving up your future?

Just now, I've suggested that you spend one day carefully taking notes of instances when, for any reason, you found yourself feeling helpless. I asked you to jot down when feelings of helplessness descended, where you were, what you were doing, with whom you were interacting . . . whatever details you might need in order to ensure that, later, when going back over that log, you'd be able to fully recall the moment.

I encouraged you to relive that moment, freeze halfway through it, and then ask yourself why you went helpless if nothing actually, objectively was present to warrant such a response.

I advised you to think about where you learned to react, in the kinds of situations you noted, with helplessness.

If you did this with attention and care—if you pondered your relived moment, tracking and exploring your feelings in that moment—I'd wager just about everything I own that you found yourself—perhaps without even at first realizing it—turned back toward your childhood.

There were your parents, telling you you're going nowhere. Teaching you you're inadequate to meet some if not all of life's main challenges. Maybe not overtly; it's unlikely you'll have memories of your parents explicitly teaching you to give up in life and constantly hand over your power. However, if you feel the truth of it, you'll soon enough see that, in one way or another, and consistently, that's exactly what was happening.

They trained you to surrender.

There's *one* kind of learned helplessness: the kind you learn from your parents. A chronic sense of helplessness is only learned; there's no other way to get it. There's no helplessness gene. *Learned* helplessness is instilled.

Every time you find yourself giving up, feeling too overwhelmed to respond at all, or in any way summarily handing off your power to people and situations you don't absolutely have to, what's happening is that you're being the dutiful child your parents once taught you to be.

You're being the adult they created.

And you *don't* have to live like that. You don't.

What you're doing when you surrender power is showing your undying love for, and loyalty to, your parents. You're proving they were right: that you really are weak; you really can't win; you really don't have what it takes.

What's it costing you to do that? *Your life.* The price for continuing to live as the person who *doesn't* measure up is everything you need to be happy.

Be realistic about what's possible for you

One of the keys to happiness in life is being realistic about life.

Sounds like such a simple thing, doesn't it? After all, life itself, in many respects, isn't the most complicated endeavor.

The primary "rules" are basic: Eat well. Get enough sleep. Be kind to others. Don't step out into moving traffic.

Mostly, the guidelines are pretty clear.

Where they tend to get messed up is when they stop being part of the outside world and start being part of your internal mind. That's where the halls of mirrors start coming into play—the warped perceptions, the scary, shadowy trails leading into dark forests and confounding labyrinths.

It's when the objective outer world turns into the subjective inner world that things start bending and pulling out of shape. A purple dog is just a purple dog—unless you're somebody who, as a child, was somehow traumatized by a purple dog. Then that dog becomes all kinds of things to you. Then it's not "just" a purple dog at all. Then it's a trigger to a whole bunch of internal stuff.

Again, I've found that a significant factor in helping someone to regain the strength their learned helplessness has led them to relinquish is showing them how to be realistic about what's possible, for him or for her.

Many people think they need to be stars. They need to be the best in their profession. They need to achieve wondrous, magnificent things. They need to be inspirational to others, superior in training and execution, unsurpassed in accomplishment, recognized for the depth and reach of their capabilities.

Hogwash. All of that is just another burden we drop on ourselves to ensure that, over and over and over, we prove we're not really "good enough."

One of life's great secrets is that good enough really *is* good enough. We don't have to be superheroes. We're not required to be awe-inspiring. We needn't be anything other than "everyday us."

Having power isn't about being exceptionally powerful. It's not about roaring through life and in every instance proving dominant and über-willful. Who has the energy? Who needs the hassle? Who wants to drive that hard?

Forget it.

Giving up your learned helplessness to get back your power just means being personally strong enough not to allow yourself to keep being hurt, maligned, and taken advantage of.

It's not about taking over the world. It's about not letting the world take over you.

(4) Gaining Back Your Power

Remembering that God made you, too!

It's easy for us to admire other people and other things. Today I went to a wooded park near my house and couldn't believe how wonderful everything was. Birds, trees, flowers, sunshine—all of it was stunning. So lovely, so awesome—in such perfect accord with God, in such harmony with his will.

When I go out into the world, or watch TV or movies, I see endless people I cannot help but admire. People who've done great things, who are *doing* great things. They've founded charitable organizations that help millions of underprivileged others. They've performed unbelievable physical feats. They have amazing talents. They're rising to life's challenges. When life has told them no, they've insisted that, instead, life change its no to *yes*.

Rousing! Galvanizing!

Worthy of high praise!

But then, when I look in the mirror, I see . . . just . . . me. Steve Arterburn.

I can't do all those things. I don't have all those skills. I can't ride a bike around the globe or lead an army to victory or be integeral to curing a terrible disease.

I'm just *Steve*.

Very often this feeling of inadequacy will creep over us if we spend too much time comparing ourselves to others. Doing so leads us, no matter how subtly, to surrender our power.

If you find yourself questioning whether you "deserve" the power that, somewhere deep inside, you know is your God-given birthright, *think* of God.

Do you think that, when God made you, his attention was somewhere else? That you were some kind of divine toss-aside—that while God formed all the "winning people" in just the way he wanted, he came up with you in a slipshod effort en route to getting somewhere he really cared about?

He didn't. God designed you with all the care and love he has for *anyone*.

God! Made! You! What else do you need to know about yourself? What other validation do you seek? What other confirmation has any meaning at all, compared to God having purposefully, willfully, and joyously created you?

You have a seat at the table. By virtue of being alive, you have all the power you could ever want, to be and do what you want.

149

What you want most of all—what anybody wants most of all—is to be happy. To be peaceful and secure and certain of God's love.

Worry no more, my friend. The fact that you're here is all you need to know about how much God loves you.

Jesus empowers the powerless

As he traveled through Galilee, he came to Cana, where he had turned the water into wine. There was a government official in nearby Capernaum whose son was very sick. When he heard that Jesus had come from Judea to Galilee, he went and begged Jesus to come to Capernaum to heal his son, who was about to die.

Jesus asked, "Will you never believe in me unless you see miraculous signs and wonders?"

The official pleaded, "Lord, please come now before my little boy dies."

Then Jesus told him, "Go back home. Your son will live!" And the man believed what Jesus said and started home.

While the man was on his way, some of his servants met him with the news that his son was alive and well. He asked them when the boy had begun to get better, and they replied, "Yesterday afternoon at one o'clock his fever suddenly disappeared!" Then the father realized that that was the very time Jesus had told him, "Your son will live." And he and his entire household believed in Jesus. This was the second miraculous sign Jesus did in Galilee after coming from Judea.

—John 4:46–54

This account, naturally enough, is frequently used to demonstrate that Jesus has power to heal the sick. And it certainly does show that. But there's another, less obvious lesson I like to contemplate whenever I think of this story: *God empowers the powerless.*

Jesus, of course, had full ability to heal *and* resurrect. He could have walked through a cemetery, waved his arms, and instantly had the biggest (if maybe the creepiest) graveyard party ever. If he'd chosen to, he could have healed everybody on the planet who had so much as the sniffles.

But he didn't, did he? He decided whom to heal.

The man who couldn't walk. The woman who managed to touch his cloak. The man born blind.

This little boy.

Here, Jesus brought to bear his powers upon a child. Not a king. Not a landowner. Not someone the world knew and admired. A sick boy. A kid who had no more earthly power than a worm.

He had no resources. No skills Jesus needed. No money to donate for the cause. No ability to procure for Jesus any votes. He couldn't give *anything*.

He was as powerless as powerless gets.

Jesus gave him back the power of his health.

Are you ready to be finished with your power outage? Jesus will reempower you. All you have to do is ask him.

No matter how powerless you might think you are, you don't lack the power to pray.

So *pray*. And then watch, as God chooses you.

Don't let Jesus die in vain: live!

Often, the people who *seemingly* want the least *actually* want the most.

I once counseled a woman, "Peggy," who, on the surface had chronic, learned helplessness. She never felt good enough. She never felt strong enough. People apparently were always taking advantage of her.

"I just can't stand up for myself," she sniffled. "No matter how hard I try not to, I always end up letting others walk all over me. Can you please help me stop letting them treat me like a doormat?"

So that's what I began endeavoring to do.

151

What I fairly quickly discovered was that Peggy *feigned* helplessness as a means of attaining power. She had mastered an art you could call "using the guise of appearing helpless in order to be passively aggressive."

You know the type. The guy who's *so* helpless, *so* weak, *so* put upon that everyone else is forever doing and being for him all the things he should be doing and being for himself. The gal who whines and moans so much about being victimized that she ends up wielding far too much power.

Surely you've known a person (or several) like this. We all have.

Here's what always lies at the bottom of that mindset: the abiding conviction that nothing, really, ever is good enough.

Not that *they* aren't good enough. They *pretend* it's all about how they're not good enough, not up to life's challenges. But dig a little deeper into what's really going on in such a person's mind, and you'll find he actually doesn't believe *life* is good enough for *him*.

He doesn't want to enter into the game of life. He's so sure life is going to let him down that he continues making sure he doesn't engage it. What he expects nothing from can't disappoint him.

In effect, he wants more. And he's not coming out to play till he gets it.

Ask yourself if you're like this, at all. Ask yourself if, in your heart of hearts, what you really want out of life is for it to prove to you somehow that it's better than you think you know it is.

If you feel any of that, remember: Jesus Christ died so *you* could live.

The God of all creation let himself be beaten, whipped, flayed, and hung up like an animal so you could be utterly, completely sure of his love for you.

Do you really think it's right for you to expect *more* out of life?

Go! Do! *Live!* This gift is from God himself. Don't return it unused.

(5) Living a Life Filled With Power

Opening yourself to God's will

A few years back I counseled Matt, a man who was buried under learned helplessness. His parents had trained him to think of himself as a nothing; his life reflected it. When I met him, he was in his late thirties and so far had done almost nothing with himself. He'd been married once, for only about a year.

"I came home from work one day," he recalled, "and she was gone. Just like in the movies. No note, no call, no offer to go to counseling. Nothing. She packed her bags and disappeared.

"And you know, the thing was, I wasn't all that surprised she was gone. She was beautiful; she was smart; she knew what she wanted out of life and was going about the hard work of getting it. What would a girl like that want with a loser like me?"

This was pretty much Matt's view of his whole relationship with existence: what would *life* want with the likes of him? So, expecting not much out, he put not much in. That's what he was getting.

When our paths crossed, Matt was at a point where he was just beginning to wonder if the only type of life he'd ever known had to be the only type of life he'd ever know.

"I want more," he said. "I think I'm just tired of feeling so power-less all the time. I'm starting to see that if I don't do something to change and improve, life will never get better. Without even realizing I was doing it, I think I've been waiting my whole life for someone else to fix it. There was always a boss who needed to give me a raise and promotion, a friend who was gonna get me that really good job, a teacher who should be giving me a good grade or getting me into a good college. It's always somebody else who is supposed to make it better. But I'm starting to see there *is* nobody else. I have to make my life better. Can you help me with that?"

"Tell you what," I said. "I can show you how your life can be everything you've ever dreamed it could be—and you *still* won't have to do it yourself. In fact, the less you do to 'make your life better,' the better your life will be."

That was the beginning of Matt's walk with Christ.

Not a year after that first encounter, guess what he was doing?

Building buildings for the poorest of the poor in Mexico. There's a team that presently has constructed, from the ground up, *fifty* orphanages, schools, homes, and care facilities for people who desperately needed them. Matt's a core member of this team.

Guess what else? Matt still hasn't learned to "take control of his life."

Thank God he hasn't.

Seeing the potential in everything

One of the most interesting things about life is how much it's *happening*. Everything we experience, everything we do, is in the present. Not before now. Not after now. *Now.*

The past is behind us; the future hasn't arrived. All we really know—all we really have—is this exact moment.

Then—whoosh!—it's gone.

Here's something to remember about the now: what's around us at any given moment is only a snapshot of an instant on the overall timeline of that thing's "life." We constantly forget this; we tend to think that what a thing is when it comes to us, when we have to relate to it or deal with it, is what it's always been. Not true! A plant will either grow or die. A new chair will sit beneath a ton of garbage one day. A candle will be gone soon enough.

And if we do that with objects, how much more so with people? For instance, when I see or engage with an elderly person, I sometimes forget there was a time when he didn't look anything like he does now. Ever seen an old photo of someone you've only known as "older," and for a second or two your brain simply has refused to believe that the teenager or twentysomething in the frame is the same retired lady you know?

You forget: she used to be young!

Just like it's so easy for us to forget that the young people we know will one day be old.

When you're plodding through life underneath learned helplessness, you really don't see the potential of things; you don't much consider what they could be or might become. Feeling powerless yourself, you're not attuned to the power of the potential all around you. When the present is all you can handle, you're basically consumed with and overwhelmed by what is; you don't have the energy or resources to ponder what was or what will be.

But when you give up learned helplessness and get back the strength it has cost you? Your perspective will widen, and you'll begin to appreciate the flow of God's power in the universe. You'll begin to comprehend things not just as they are in a moment but also, for example, how they were before you came across them and what they possibly or surely will become.

Suddenly, that's not just an old man: he's a whole person, with a history and a future, whom you're noticing in one particular instant.

That's not just a little girl; she's an old woman who hasn't happened yet.

When you gain back for yourself the power God wants all his followers to have, you move closer to being like Jesus. Jesus sees everything in terms of eternity. While none of us can do that completely, we sure can taste it. And it's mighty sweet indeed.

Fixing the potholes in your own life

Before we switch focus, I want to say a few practical-sense words about what it really *means* to regain life-power. That's where you find the true joy of giving up helplessness and getting back strength.

It's true and needful that people endeavoring to grow spiritually and psychologically deal with plenty of abstracts. What's my proper relationship to God? How do I know he's really there? How can I be sure Jesus died for my personal sins? And so on.

Those are crucial concerns, questions to which we all must seek answers.

But knowing God, experiencing the reality of God, giving up learned helplessness to gain the power God has longed for you to claim as your own also offers a veritable world of real-time, immediate, concrete pleasures that can provide positive feelings more affirming than are available anywhere else.

Having God in your heart means having God in your life. When you have God in your life, your life gets a *lot* better. And not just metaphysically, either.

What makes Jesus so inexpressibly inspiring is that he became fully human. This means we can be sure that he knew, as God knows we know, what it actually means to live, work, and strive in this, our physical world.

Just *thinking*, right now, about all the things I need to take care of in my home alone is fairly staggering. Kitchen sink needs caulking. So does master-bedroom shower enclosure. Our ant problem, if not soon solved, is going to cause either our starvation or our moving away. Some entryway tiles are loose. A few knobs are about to wobble out of their doors. The water heater occasionally sounds like it's in the midst of a drive-by shooting.

Goes on and on.

And you know what? I'm not concerned about any of it.

I have God in my life. I have Jesus *the carpenter* in my soul.

That Jesus isn't lazy. He isn't afraid to do the pragmatic, everyday things that must get done if we're to live lives worthy of his sacrifice on our behalf.

That Jesus knows how to roll up his sleeves and take care of business. In his name I am, to say the least, pleased to do the same.

Yes, God is in his heaven. And yes, seated at his side is Jesus himself—the Prince of Peace, the holy Redeemer of the sins of all humankind.

I know, too, that Jesus is as close to me as that big screen-hole in the window of my boy's bedroom.

Next time you feel like saying "I can't" or "Yes but . . . ," resist; restrain yourself. With God on the inside, you'll be stunned at all you can do—how far you can go—in the world.

Questions for Discussion

1. When was the last time you felt yourself to be powerless? Were you, in fact, powerless—or was there something going on right then that made you feel so?

2. Do you feel you've often allowed feelings of powerlessness to stymie your development? Can you give an example of that?

3. Do you think your parents taught you anything about yourself, or your life, that's led you (occasionally or usually) to feel more powerless than you actually are? Can you think of an instance of how they conveyed this to you?

4. Do you think you sometimes have such high self-expectations that, instead of feeling inspired by your aspirations, you feel discouraged and even defeated? Can you give a real-life illustration of that?

5. Do you ever feel you're left out, even a little, from the empowering grace of Jesus? That others are more gifted, more successful, more talented, more worthy? If you do sometimes feel that way, how do you come back out of that funk?

6. Do you find that knowing Jesus, or being inspired by him, carries all the way into inspiration for even the most mundane chores and tasks? If not, why not? If so, how does this work and feel for you?

7

Give Up Isolation;
Get Back Connection and Community

(1) What Is Isolation?

Keeping alone

Marilyn, one of my favorite people in the office, looked deeply troubled.

"Steve," she said. "Can I talk to you a minute?"

"Of course. Come on in. What's going on?"

"It's my dad." Instantly, tears welled up in her eyes. "He took a fall."

"Oh no. Is he all right?"

"He is. It wasn't a big deal. But this isn't the first time it's happened. He fell in a parking lot less than two weeks ago. And I guess the other day he fell in his home's entryway."

"How do you mean, you 'guess' he fell? Do you not know?"

"Well, that's the thing," she continued. "That's what has me so upset. He lives alone. And I mean, *really* alone. Ever since my step-mother, June, died—they were married about thirty-five years—he's been completely isolated.

"And he wasn't exactly Mr. Social before that. June was pretty much the only person my dad ever saw. He retired at fifty-five. Now he's seventy-eight; his wife has been gone five years; he doesn't know any of his neighbors. He's a complete shut-in."

"Well, he has you," I offered. "And you have a brother, don't you?"

"That's right; it's me and my brother. But he lives all the way in Hawaii. I'm here in California. And our dad lives in Maryland. We almost couldn't live any farther from one another."

"Wow. I didn't know your family was so spread apart."

"We're as far apart as we could be—geographically *and* emotionally. It's because of my dad that we're like this. Growing up, he just refused to have anything to do with us.

"And he's still that way. He *never* writes or calls us; he barely—I mean, *barely*—acknowledges our letters or calls to him. The only reason I even know he's been falling lately is, the guy who does his lawn found him after the last one. He was sitting on his front porch, hurt; the man went inside, found our numbers in my dad's address book, and called us."

Marilyn started to cry again. "I can't go visit him; he won't let me. My brother won't go; he says that since Dad wasn't there for him then, he's not going to be there for him now.

"I just don't know what to do, Steve. My dad's so alone. He won't let anybody help him or care for him—or just *be* there with him. And it's just tearing me up inside."

This story sharply captures why self-isolation is such a terribly hurtful thing. I don't mean for the person who's isolating (though it's surely doing him zero good). I mean for everyone else who cares about him.

No matter how much we try to convince ourselves of the contrary, the final truth is that no one on this planet is truly alone.

John Donne probably said it best:

> No man is an island, entire of itself; every man
> is a piece of the continent, a part of the main.
> If a clod be washed away by the sea, Europe
> is the less, as well as if a promontory were, as
> well as if a manor of thy friend's or of thine
> own were: any man's death diminishes me,
> because I am involved in mankind,
> and therefore never send to know for whom
> the bells tolls; it tolls for thee.

Never committing emotionally

"Ken" is the nicest guy around. He has a wonderfully wry sense of humor (he always lends sharp observations; he's king of the witty aside). As a history professor at a state college, he has lots of people in his life: regular faculty meetings and functions, students constantly waiting outside his office, and of course, filled-to-bursting classrooms.

A French-fluent Francophile who's vacationed annually in France for three decades, Ken's also an excellent cook. Once a month or so he home-hosts big dinner parties in which he treats friends and family to whatever new dish he's been mastering since the last affair.

Must be a reasonably happy guy, right?

Wrong.

For all of that—and for everything else Ken is and does—the man will not commit to anything emotionally. He *is* wry; that slightly cynical, always-on-the-outside mode of engagement ongoingly keeps him at a comfortable distance from whatever's really happening right around him.

As with everyone who's known Ken for any length of time, it took me a while to catch on to his life-approach. The more I got

161

to know him, and the more I hung out with him and his wife, the more I realized that when it comes to connecting with anything that involves emotions, Ken simply stops.

He'll acknowledge that it's his wedding anniversary. However, he won't make any plans in that regard, and he won't act particularly pleased (or displeased) when his wife does.

He'll attend his son's birthday party—the one his wife put together, because he would no sooner be part of that than he would jump from an airplane—and he'll even make a contribution to the little pile of presents. But Ken's package will be the only one still in the bag of the store from which it was purchased. He doesn't wrap gifts; that would feel like truly engaging.

Those dinner parties? Yes, he cooks the (always delicious) meals. Throughout the evening, though, he merely sits back in his chair, sips wine, and makes what generally amount to (you guessed it) wry asides.

Over time, I saw how *un*happy Ken really was. He had a block that kept him from giving up his isolation to get back connection and community. The block, it turned out, was fear, born out of his pain from having his mother suddenly die in an accident when he was very young. Desperate to stop hurting, and terrified he never would, he froze his feelings and learned to never, ever invest emotionally.

It's possible to seem connected with others, to seem to be communing with family, friends, and neighbors, while actually being more isolated than a mountain hermit.

Do you, more often than you know is healthy, find yourself staying aloof, disengaging, making sure others are aware that your contribution to life's dialogue will be the occasional erudite remark or humorous observation?

If so, you're sacrificing real connection with others for your own perceived protection.

And there's nothing funny about that at all.

Feeling that only you know what's best and right

If there's one thing "Pam" knows, it's that she knows everything. She has an answer for any question that ever surfaces. If one of her kids has a problem at school, if a friend has an issue at work, if an acquaintance is struggling with a personal difficulty—anyone, anything—then Pam will know what's best and right for everyone involved to do.

Barely matters whether anyone's asked her, either. She'll put forth the truth; she doesn't wait to be invited to have an opinion. Pam's so certain that the pure facthood of what she says will be immediately obvious to all hearers that it'll go without saying that "interfering" was best.

She's right: it does go without saying. Must, because no one ever says it.

When I was seated with Pam at a luncheon, also at our table was "Denise," a realtor who was sharing a frustrating problem with the impact new government regulations were having on the processing of homeowner loans. I didn't really understand it, but two others there likewise were in real estate, and they seemed to catch on. I sipped my water, listened . . . and started to daydream, which I tend to do when I can't quite fathom things around me.

"Well, know what you should do?" piped up Pam. *That* got my attention.

I know Pam. Unless she's secretly been taking night classes in the economics of real estate, she knows no more about that universe of business than I do. She owns a children's clothing store. It's occupied the same (adorable) little cottage for *thirty years*.

Pam wouldn't know an amortized mortgage yield from a pair of infant overalls. But sure enough, she waded right into bottomless waters, confident that the sheer quality of her intellect would prevail. Nope.

Fortunately, these folks were a civilized bunch, and they didn't overtly let on that they'd just realized they were lunching with a crazy person.

Pam's *not* a crazy person. But she is someone who's found and cultivated a way—and, sadly, not an all-that-uncommon way—to isolate herself even while seeming, from a distance, to be every-which-way connected.

Pam doesn't know everything. Nevertheless, she essentially insists that she does by fronting an attitude of such intrusive finality that people end up more than happy to hear her out, smile, thank her, and move on.

Then Pam is, yet again, right back where she started: the smartest, loneliest woman around.

(2) What Isolation Does to Your Life

Keeps you "safe"

"I've lived in this house eighty years," said "Belle," a woman I'd come to know through my church. Her home, which I was visiting for the first time, was exceptionally neat and clean. Almost like a museum. Not because it held objects of art, though, or anything really remarkable; rather, because every single item looked as if it had been placed *exactly* where it was and rarely if ever got moved, touched, or breathed on.

The vase was precisely in the center of the side table. The *TV Guide* was squared with the edge of the television's top. The coffee table display pieces were just exactly so. The mantel's candlesticks were evenly spaced to the thirty-second of an inch. Everything said, "The inhabitant cannot abide disorder. Do. Not. Disturb."

I liked it. I *like* order! I feel that any room I so much as pass through falls into instantaneous disarray. Here was Belle, ninety-two, who clearly vacuumed and dusted daily, if not every fifteen minutes. And my visit had come up unexpectedly. This was how she actually *lived*.

"Really?" I marveled. "You've been here eighty years?"

"Sure have," she said proudly. "My family moved into this house when I was twelve. Lived here ever since."

I knew from mutual friends that, until four years prior, Belle's younger sister had lived with her.

Belle, I knew, had never married. Her sister hadn't either.

"That *is* a long time." I tried to say it in a way that would let her know if she were up for talking, I'd certainly be interested in listening to her story.

She wasn't, though. What I learned, in the hour or so I spent with her that day, is that Belle didn't really want to talk with anyone. What she'd done for herself, I realized, was create a world so devoid of outside influence that she nearly might as well have been cryogenically preserved in dioramic display.

"Mid-Twentieth-Century Elderly White Woman's House," the prominent placard might have read. "Notice the doilies."

As a person who in many ways has made a life's work out of discerning and examining the various means by which people arrange to keep themselves isolated (be it from others, from Jesus, even from themselves), I knew that, in Belle, I'd found someone remarkably distinguished—perhaps unsurpassed.

Ninety-two years old. One place, eight decades. Ever single.

No dog. No cat. No great-grandkids running around. No neighbors swinging by.

No picture album to show you. No photos of anyone on any of the walls.

There was a moment when Belle stepped into her flawless little kitchen to make us tea that, very briefly, I wept at the sadness of it.

Here was a woman who'd taken so many pains to keep herself safe that she'd never lived at all.

Never having to adjust for anyone else

Now and then I'm honored to be called upon for marriage counseling with young couples set on taking that big walk down the aisle. It's a facet of ministry that I relish; I love talking with an engaged pair about what they'd do well to consider as they move closer and closer to life-defining commitment.

Of all the things I say at that stage of their relationship, I think the most important is a little speech that runs something like this.

What makes marriage such a blessing from God—what makes it so special, so wonderful, so important—is that it provides you the greatest means possible for personal growth and development.

Know why? In a marriage, you *must* adjust. When you marry, a part of the pact that the pastor doesn't say is, what you've just signed up to do, every single day, in one way or another, is *adjust*.

Up until the time that you're married, you're the ship's captain. If you want to be in a bad mood for no particular reason, there isn't anything to stop you from complaining and moaning until your voice gives out. You can grouse around, kick things, curse, and generally be just as grumpy as you wish.

The moment you're part of a married couple, this radically changes. Then you're no longer free at all to simply be and do whatever you want, however you want, with whomever you want.

You're then part of a relationship—one based on love. And when you love somebody, what you want is for him or her to have the best possible experiences that it's within your power to provide.

Grumping and grousing won't get that for her. That won't make him happy. That won't make her feel good. He won't *like* that. Nobody does.

So what do you do? You dig down deep, and you change. You *don't* fuss, punch things, throw little tantrums. Instead, you compel yourself to do what only you can make yourself do.

You grow up. You mature. You start examining those inner dynamics that drive you to act in ways that compromise the life-experience of your spouse. You find those things—things you'd likely never have found if love itself hadn't been motivating you to dig deep enough to find them—and you change them.

In a word, love makes you *grow*. Being in communion with another drives you to develop, to become patient—and, ultimately, to gain wisdom. It's not the only great thing about marriage, but it's right up there with the best of them.

If you're isolated, though? If you never need to adjust what you think, the ways you act, the filters through which you perceive reality, the habits and decisions of the person you were (if you're married) the day you said "I do"?

Then good luck to you. Because "luck" is about the only avenue via which you're likely ever to know true, sustained happiness.

Increasingly out of touch

We've seen repeatedly that our world moves fast. Nothing and nowhere moves as fast as does the world of communications. You might not see even this book as a "book."

Maybe you're reading on your phone. Or your laptop. Perhaps you don't need a laptop anymore because you have an amazing little device whose name starts with a small "i." Could be that by the time this gets released, e-readers and tablets will be *so* yesterday. For all I know, you're hearing me with your portable hologram transporting unit or modular optivision descrambling card.

Yeah, I made those up. But they sound about right. Because who *knows?*

One thing I do know for sure: if you live in isolation—if you live in such a way as to rarely if ever communicate with others—then before long at all you *will* become out of touch with how people are communicating. At all.

I used to have a radio show. I still have it and, God willing, I always will. But it's not just a radio show anymore! (What am I, a caveman?) *New Life Live* now is broadcast, for example, online and on digital TV. We've done what we must do—what anyone must do if he wants to continue being "part of the conversation." We change, and keep changing, the ways we connect.

I must admit I'm hardly what you'd call a communications savant. In fact, if I had my way, we'd all go back to an era when conversation meant actually *being* with a person. In certain respects, I'm still getting used to the *telephone*. And here I am now, in an age when (as I read today in one of the nation's few remaining newspapers) people no longer want to abide the inconvenience of e-mail; *that* just *takes* too long!

Maybe this isn't surprising to anyone but me. That wouldn't change the cold, hard fact, though, that—hide though I might want to—I can't afford *not* to find out what kinds of media technologies currently are replacing e-mail.

I either keep up and meet the world where it's at, or the world will pass me by. And that'd be a terrible shame.

Because what's in the world? *People.*

And what do people do? Communicate with other people!

When they do, I want to be right there with them, getting my share of the sharing.

(Now, if only I were smart enough not to keep losing my smart-phone.)

(3) How to Give Up Isolation

Think about why you isolate

It's commonly accepted that one of the worst situations in prison is being put into solitary confinement. But have you ever considered what it is, exactly, that makes having to do time in solitary so harrowing?

Why is this "Warden Weapon Number One"? What's so bad about isolation that even hardened, veteran inmates shudder to think of facing it? Is being left alone *that* horrific?

Matter of fact, it is.

Scientists and psychologists have long been aware of the acute suffering caused by removing a person from all contact with other people. The need to socialize, interact, and simply engage with others is so intrinsic a part of human nature—it's hardwired into what we are—that eliminating the possibility of talking and of shared experiences is among the most damaging things you can do to a person.

That's how social we're designed to be: it's a profound torture to remove from a person the presence of others. You force a man to be alone, and you're causing almost as much anguish to him as is possible.

Consider this, too: study after study shows that most people fear public speaking more than they do death.

More than *death*! Again, this speaks to how deeply we're wired to care about nothing in this world so much as we do our relationship with others.

The point I'd like to make here is how unnatural it is for anyone to isolate himself. While physical isolation—of the solitary confinement sort—is the most dramatic kind, emotional isolation can be just as damaging. That's why it's so critical that, if you're isolated, physically or emotionally, you take great care to think about why.

What happened? Who are you so angry with that now you don't want to deal with anyone? Who put it into your mind that the best way to go through life is alone?

Isolation is *the* most unnatural thing in existence. If you're isolating, or have a strong tendency to do so, there's a cause. Something, somewhere in your past, went wrong.

Pray for God to show you what this something is. Seek the help of a good Christian counselor.

Isolate *that* thing, and renounce it in the name of Jesus Christ.

Then pick up the phone and call someone. Go outside. Join a group. *Enjoy life the way God intended: in the company of others.*

Consider the true costs of remaining alone

"Lisa" wasn't a shut-in, insofar as she was contracts attorney for one of California's largest municipal land-use agencies. So she did get out of her apartment every morning. But even at the office building, her spot was *way* down in the basement, as far away from everyone else as could be achieved.

Lisa wasn't, to put it a certain way, a pleasant person.

She complained about everything. It had to be how she thought it ought to be, or she'd act to make sure that it was. That's part of why she became a lawyer: she loved to argue. She was a contracts lawyer because the only thing she liked more than arguing was nit-picking over details.

The perfect person to pore over your agreements! (and disagreements).

Because of her personality—frankly—Lisa was nearly as isolated as someone with an out-of-home career can be. Her office was remote; no one wanted to deal with her. And while there, others isolated Lisa. At home, she did a fine job of this herself. Once back in her apartment, she almost never left.

Finally, a pastor and I decided to try a little tough love. Nothing else was working. Lisa was forty-six; she was approaching genuine obesity; there hadn't been a man in her life for some twenty years.

"Look at you," I said as she sat in the huge living room lounge chair where she practically lived. "Look at your life. You know no one. No one knows you. You're single and on track to spend the rest of your life that way.

"You only work and watch TV. That's it. No friends. No family you talk with. No boyfriend. No dates. You've made a complete hermit of yourself. And you've been in so many fights with so many colleagues that finally they jammed you into a dinky little windowless hole.

"Of course you hate it down there; it's a *cell*! But you got put there because you're so difficult to deal with. That's why co-workers who make half as much have ocean-overlooking offices while you're in a janitor's closet.

"When you come home, you plop yourself down in front of this idiot box and vegetate for six hours. Then you haul yourself over to bed, sleep, and wake just to restart that same miserable loop.

"*No more.* Isolating is costing you too much, Lisa. It's costing your *life.* You need to get your life back.

"I'm coming here tomorrow morning; I'm picking you up; I'm taking you to church. I don't care if you think religion or spirituality is stupid—that's what we're doing. If you aren't ready to go at ten, I may be the last person in your life who's not on television."

So that's what I did. And Lisa did come with me that morning.

That was several years ago.

Today? Today, Lisa loves the ocean view from her office.

Baby steps

We humans are creatures of habit. Once we've used a toothpaste brand, for instance, *that* (assuming we liked it) becomes ours. No other paste or gel will do. We'd rather brush with earwax than with *another* kind of toothpaste.

Whether or not that's a bit much, you get the point: we like what we like, and we do what we do. Once we're in any kind of behavioral pattern, getting out can be a true challenge.

Goethe once said, "Habit is a man's sole comfort. We dislike doing without even unpleasant things to which we have become accustomed."

Well, there's nothing more unpleasant than being isolated—even if at the time we don't realize it. When we come to understand that perpetual isolation is causing us to lead a life that's actually no life at all, we tend to want, somehow, to change it.

But how, exactly, to go about this? If you've kept yourself this long from the presence and company of others, how do you re-initiate the connection and community God intends for your enrichment? It's one thing to say, "I'm going out there to start living a rich life that involves caring for and being cared for by others." It's quite another to really put together for yourself an existence radically different from what you've long been experiencing.

If you've decided to come out of hiding, may I suggest that you not start by, say, running for political office or auditioning for the lead in a musical? It's more likely you'll have lasting, life-reshaping success if you go about it like a sculptor molds a lump of clay into a statue: *carefully, slowly, patiently.*

Depending on just how isolated you've been—and how hesitant you are to get back out and actually engage—do something at first that, relative to your situation, is simple. Attend a public lecture. Go to a library. Take a class in something—perhaps even a one-day session where you're basically sitting with others and taking notes. Do something where you're out in the world, with people you don't know, doing something basic together.

Try this once. No one says you should emerge on your first day and administrate a parade.

For now, just step into the parade that's already happening. Step in anywhere—then start walking along with everyone else. Pretty soon you'll hear the music. You'll relax.

You'll enjoy being included in the procession.

> Let us think of ways to motivate one another to acts of love and good works. And let us not neglect our meeting together, as some people do, but encourage one another, especially now that the day of his return is drawing near.
>
> —Hebrews 10:24–25

(4) Gaining Back Connection and Community

God calls us to community

One of the saddest things happening right now is the way so many are deciding they'd rather go it alone than continue attending church.

Everywhere you look, there seems to be another report or story about how people are leaving their congregations. Memberships of most mainline denominations are down. General attendance itself is down. More and more folks who've always gone are becoming "unchurched."

Now, granted, much of the "news" that centers on how bad things are for Christianity in America comes from sources with a lot invested in drumming up fear and controversy. "Things Pretty Much Continuing as Usual" wouldn't garner much attention. A dependable audience is essential if you're going to sell ad space/time to the businesses who'd like your followers to buy what they're selling. You gotta have traffic to make money.

The best way to retain an audience? Scare or upset them. Then, invested in the drama, they'll stay around or keep returning to see how it's unfolding.

When I read headlines, then, like "Churches Fading Away!" I take them with a grain of salt. I know things aren't all bad. Many, many thousands of churches are doing just fine.

But I also know that a lot of the data emerging lately has been accurate. Church attendance *is* down. Membership numbers *have* dropped. We *are* losing parishioners.

And that breaks my heart.

God wants us to live in communion. We're not to lose our connection with others, our understanding of ourselves as part of a larger whole that serves as God's body on earth. God designed us to be social creatures because he doesn't want any of us—not one of us—to isolate.

Look at Paul's words in Romans 12:3–8:

Because of the privilege and authority God has given me, I give each of you this warning: Don't think you are better than you really are. Be honest in your evaluation of yourselves, measuring yourselves by the faith God has given us. Just as our bodies have many parts and

173

each part has a special function, so it is with Christ's body. We are many parts of one body, and we all belong to each other.

In his grace, God has given us different gifts for doing certain things well. So if God has given you the ability to prophesy, speak out with as much faith as God has given you. If your gift is serving others, serve them well. If you are a teacher, teach well. If your gift is to encourage others, be encouraging. If it is giving, give generously. If God has given you leadership ability, take the responsibility seriously. And if you have a gift for showing kindness to others, do it gladly.

Many people have forgotten this most basic of human imperatives. Don't be one of them.

Get out there and be a part of the body of Christ, as God intended.

Love unshared is no love at all

One of the teachers of religious law was standing there listening to the debate. He realized that Jesus had answered well, so he asked, "Of all the commandments, which is the most important?"

Jesus replied, "The most important commandment is this: 'Listen, O Israel! The Lord our God is the one and only Lord. And you must love the Lord your God with all your heart, all your soul, all your mind, and all your strength.' The second is equally important: 'Love your neighbor as yourself.' No other commandment is greater than these."

The teacher of religious law replied, "Well said, Teacher. You have spoken the truth by saying that there is only one God and no other. And I know it is important to love him with all my heart and all my understanding and all my strength, and to love my neighbor as myself. This is more important than to offer all of the burnt offerings and sacrifices required in the law."

Realizing how much the man understood, Jesus said to him, "You are not far from the Kingdom of God." And after that, no one dared to ask him any more questions.

—Mark 12:28–34

One of my favorite parts about this, the Greatest Commandment passage, is its final sentence: "After that, no one dared to ask him any more questions."

Mark's statement nails the finality with which those who heard Jesus proclaim the mandate understood it. It points to how we should hear it, too. No argument. No retort. No further definitions necessary.

Love your neighbor as yourself.

Boom. There's nothing else to talk about.

God said it, and you'd better believe it.

Unfortunately, I could make a strong case to say that the person who isolates has a very dim view of life in Christ. To put it in strong terms, the Christian who's alone isn't much of a Christian.

Jesus didn't say to think about loving your neighbor. He didn't suggest that loving your neighbor is a decent idea. He didn't recommend sending out loving prayers for your neighbor.

His dictum is clear: *love.* As a *verb.* That's active, hands-on, go-and-see-if-your-neighbor-has-any-needs love.

You can't love your neighbor if you don't know him.

And you can't know him if you never leave your house.

Go, Christian! *Be* Christian. Love your neighbor, as you love yourself.

Love your neighbor now, as God, through Jesus, has showed how much he loves you.

With God, you've already got company

The most important thing to remember about giving up isolation to gain back connection and community is that being isolated really is an illusion.

You might sense that you're alone. It might feel like there's nobody else in this whole wide world who even knows you're alive. You might feel so cut off that when you so much as open the blinds you wonder if you've just inadvertently issued a hundred house-party invitations.

You might, in every way, perceive that you're as alone as alone gets. That's a delusion. *Nobody* is alone. You could leave your friends and family, pack your bags, fly to Africa, hike two hundred miles into the Sahara, dig down twenty feet, crawl inside . . . and you'd still no more be alone than you'd be if you did throw that big soirée.

God lets no person be alone.

Not here. Not there. Not anywhere.

You've already got company. Might as well send out the rest of the invites. No use holding back now, right?

If you doubt whether or not you're really alone in this world, read carefully, one by one, each word of Psalm 139 (verses 1–18).

Don't skip. Don't skim. Read.

> O Lord, you have examined my heart
> and know everything about me.
> You know when I sit down or stand up.
> You know my thoughts even when I'm far away.
> You see me when I travel
> and when I rest at home.
> You know everything I do.
> You know what I am going to say
> even before I say it, Lord.
> You go before me and follow me.
> You place your hand of blessing on my head.
> Such knowledge is too wonderful for me,
> too great for me to understand!
>
> I can never escape from your Spirit!
> I can never get away from your presence!
> If I go up to heaven, you are there;
> if I go down to the grave, you are there.
> If I ride the wings of the morning,
> if I dwell by the farthest oceans,
> even there your hand will guide me,
> and your strength will support me.

I could ask the darkness to hide me
    and the light around me to become night—
        but even in darkness I cannot hide from you.
To you the night shines as bright as day.
    Darkness and light are the same to you.

You made all the delicate, inner parts of my body
    and knit me together in my mother's womb.
Thank you for making me so wonderfully complex!
    Your workmanship is marvelous—how well I know it.
You watched me as I was being formed in utter seclusion,
    as I was woven together in the dark of the womb.
You saw me before I was born.
    Every day of my life was recorded in your book.
Every moment was laid out
    before a single day had passed.

How precious are your thoughts about me, O God.
    They cannot be numbered!
I can't even count them;
    they outnumber the grains of sand!
And when I wake up,
    you are still with me!

(5) Living a Life Filled With Connection and Community

Reaching out to others

A man I knew, "Cliff," was so secluded that *finding* his abode took me about two days.

Not that I was wandering in a literal forest or anything. But Cliff did live in a mobile-home park, one with so many numberless units packed into such a bizarrely networked web of twisting side routes that, when trying to navigate, you half expect to come across an abandoned UPS or FedEx truck that never made it back out (and you start suspecting you won't reemerge either).

Wanting to visit him, yet failing to locate anything like the address he'd mentioned, I tried a second time.

Foiled again.

I phoned from somewhere on the development's periphery.

"What *is* it with this place?" I complained. "I feel like a mouse in a maze—only I'm an amusing experiment and there's no actual cheese. Help!"

Cliff chuckled and agreed to shoot up a flare (in essence).

When I finally arrived, I understood why he was where he was. Cliff, who'd been the ultimate recluse, was very thin; he had a flowing gray beard; he wore clothes from the thrift store he scavenged for virtually everything he had; he ate only what little he'd buy at a farmer's market.

Cliff was constantly, completely unplugged.

"You need to get out more," I said. "You need to get out *ever*."

"What do you think I should do?" he asked. I was extremely touched by his earnestness: through prayer and counseling, Cliff, now in his early sixties, had recently decided he needed to give up isolation and regain his long-lost sense of connection, of community.

"I might know just the thing," I answered.

As it turns out, I did.

About a week after I introduced Cliff to the executive director of an amazing social services/nonprofit organization, Cliff was the volunteer in charge of its food pantry. Ever since, he's been serving in that crucial capacity for about thirty hours a week.

Oh, and did I mention: my friend Cliff is one of the most respected classical philosophers in America. His papers and books are devoured by intellectuals all over the planet.

That wasn't enough, however, for this erstwhile loner.

It couldn't be.

Until a man learns to reach out to others, his life, to him, cannot possibly feel fulfilled.

Jesus commanded us to love others, just like we love ourselves.

Cliff learned that lesson; last time I spoke with him, he sounded happier, by far, than he has at any time in the long while I've known him.

Have you learned that same lesson? And are you *proving* that you have?

Harnessing the power of others

True brilliance is a rare enough commodity. I would, in fact, go so far as to say that if in the course of your life you ever meet one bona fide genius, you can count yourself blessed indeed.

Today we're quite free with the word "genius." But I'm not free with it at all. I've actually *known* one. If ever you get this opportunity, you'll realize how rare and precious such people are.

Allen was one of the most articulate guys *ever*. There was almost no subject he couldn't introduce, explain, and summarize with a spontaneous dissertation that left no doubt he was profoundly well-informed. Honestly, it didn't seem possible that Allen had ever been exposed to any info he'd forgotten. A constitutional inability to *not* remember seemed perhaps the only explanation for why he apparently did know everything.

That, and he read as though he were starving and words were food.

Intaking, processing, and then expressing every kind of information and idea you've ever imagined is where Allen's prodigious talent *began*. He was also a mind-blowing writer. One of the globe's most sought-after freelance magazine journalists, Allen had been published in nearly every major source in the U.S. He'd been almost everywhere on earth, and he'd met and interviewed just about anyone who wielded commercial or political power.

This was a man who "had it all." His address book could have belonged to our nation's president. There wasn't a book publisher in the country that didn't want anything he cared to write.

None of this was even close to enough for Allen.

"I'm tired of working for others," he confided one night over dinner. "I want to start my own project."

"What are you thinking of doing?" I asked. Though I hadn't the slightest notion what he might be referring to, I already was excited about it.

"I want to start a magazine—one that takes time to deal with the truly significant issues of the day, instead of primarily purposing to provide advertising fodder. I want to do thoughtful pieces that truly explore, that do intellectual and emotional justice to the most important things happening today. A magazine where the subject matter and words make a difference."

"Sounds *great*," I said. "Do it. I might invest!"

"Thanks." He paused. "But what I need from you is guidance. Here's why: I've never *not* worked alone. I travel alone; I develop my sources alone; I research alone; I write alone. Everything I do is alone. But if I'm going to do this, I'm going to have to reacquaint myself with what it means to work with others: to listen to them, to consider them, to make sure they're part of the process that in many ways I've always owned myself.

"Can you help me, Steve? Can you help me learn how to harness the power of others?"

Slowly but surely, Allen learned how to do exactly that: how to forge a team from disparate individuals, how to bring them along in a jointly creative process, how to navigate them and encourage them toward the fulfillment of a shared vision, one that would never be born of and emerge from just one soul.

Mostly, my friend Allen learned to discover, cultivate, and appreciate the power of others. I know for a fact that he's never been happier.

He's been publishing his magazine for five years now, and he's making it when many others are not.

The last time I spoke with Allen, he said, "I used to always laugh at how corny the saying was, 'There's no "i" in team.' But you know what, Steve? I don't laugh at that anymore. Now it's the central saying of my life."

Make sure it's yours, too.

If you aren't on a team, *join* one. If you don't find a team you'd like to join, then *start* one.

The very best of what you can do alone pales in comparison to what you can do in communion with others.

Participating in God's "broader life"

Again, there's truly no "i" in "team." Where there *is* an "i," though, is in "isolation." (Yeah, yeah, *two*. Which just makes my point twice as strong!)

In the end, isolation isn't really about anything so much as self-ishness and ego gratification. I know that's awfully harsh, and in some legitimate ways, it's too unforgiving. I certainly don't mean to dismiss the real and unfortunate reasons so many people have for turning inward instead of connecting with others and healthily participating in their community.

Nobody isolates because he feels good about who he is. And rarely does anyone learn to feel bad about himself anywhere but from his parents. A person trained to think poorly of himself or herself deserves our compassion.

Even so: when you isolate, you're revealing and confirming that, deep down, you don't think anything is more important than you. Nobody's concerns compare. Nobody's needs can compete. Nobody's worldview is as sound and reasonable.

Nobody else knows, or can comprehend, the trouble you've seen.

Basically, you remain alone because way, way deep inside, you believe that yours is the only company worth keeping.

Then you get the world you choose. Yours.

Your walls. Your floor. Your ceiling.

Your little box.

181

And here's God, waiting for you to come out and play. You may have a small life; you may, by isolating, be doing virtually everything you can to ensure your life remains as limited as you possibly can preserve it. But *God* doesn't have a small life. Doesn't isolate. Doesn't withdraw. Doesn't decide "the world outside" isn't sufficiently compelling and important to engage.

God *is* the outside! God's everywhere, always, doing everything. Period.

And you think you'll hide from God? You'll isolate away from him? It would be easier to hide from your own skin.

God wants you to be your happiest, healthiest self; he wants you to give up lonely disconnection and get back vital community. And he's provided you with every means of doing that. He's made it so simple and straightforward for you to enter into and savor life's big, bright, bold beauty—which he's always, everywhere orchestrating— that all you have to do to receive full membership and benefits and privileges is one, single, itty-bitty little thing.

Ask.

That's it. Ask God to deliver you from your isolation and to invite you into communion with him—and through him, with others.

Just knock, fellow learner, and the door will be opened.

Questions for Discussion

1. Do you isolate? If so, why? What brings you out of it? If nothing has brought you out of it so far, what will be the answer?

2. Have you ever experienced drawing out into the world a truly isolated person? What was this like? How did he/she respond to your efforts?

3. Do you know anyone who uses a busy social or work life to isolate? Pretends to be engaging the world but really keeps all else at bay? Have you ever been able to break through to reach him/her? How did that go?

4. What (if any) role in your own life is played by God's call to all his believers to join in community with other followers? Does communing in this way come naturally to you? Why or why not, do you think? If not, what can you do about it?

5. Talk about an experience when you were part of a team whose members accomplished more together than any could have alone.

8

Give Up Addiction; Get Back Freedom

(1) What Is Addiction?

The dependent life

Over much time I've come to believe there are three kinds of people when it comes to the problem of addiction: those who have themselves been addicts; those who've loved and been very close to addicts; and those so fortunate as to never have had addiction be so imminently a part of their lives, either way.

Guess which group is *by far* the smallest.

Everybody at least knows someone—and it's almost always someone close—who's wrestled with this demon. Addiction, I'm convinced, is the most widespread malady in and throughout today's culture except overeating, which in some cases results from addiction. Liquor, pornography, pot, harder drugs, nicotine: these and many more temptations are everywhere you go, just waiting for you to indulge in them a little. So that you can indulge in them a little more. And then a bit more. And then just one more time.

Somewhere along that line, you stop controlling your desire for whatever has you hooked, and desire starts controlling you. And you probably won't even be aware of when that switch has occurred, because it will be so gradual, over such a long stretch. It might be years and years before you recognize it's even happened at all—until you've lost your friends, your family, your job, and everything else you hold dear.

Then you might begin wondering if you had or have an addiction. Sometimes even that sort of desperate condition isn't enough to convince the addict that he's lost control of his life. It's astonishing, for some, how much further down "bottom" can keep dropping.

What the addict has such difficulty realizing, at just about any point along the trajectory of addiction, is the degree to which he's traded control for feeding the monster. The full-blown addict cares only about getting that next fix, that next high, that next rush that comes from embracing the temptation.

Eventually, your experience is simply that you're just too weak to resist.

Of course, you *try* to resist. You try to say the last time you ate that giant sundae, or watched that porno clip, or pounded that mixed drink, was *the* last time. You're going to be strong *this* time—stronger than you've ever been.

You convince yourself that when temptation next comes along, you'll turn your back, snub it, ignore it, rise above the challenge. You might even convince somebody else you'll do that—that you've changed.

You thought that after the last time you succumbed.

You'll think it after the next time, too.

If you are or know one, you don't need me to tell you that an addict doesn't go through life wondering when and how he'll get his next fix.

Getting his next fix *is* an addict's life.
And that's no life at all.

Not *as overt as you might think*

It's easy enough to think of the addict as some wild-eyed, strung-out figure lurking and even residing in alleyways, committing endless crimes to feed his horrific habit. That's the image the media largely give us.

While, tragically, a lot of people addicted to hard drugs do live a life of squalor and ugliness, addiction nevertheless comes in many, many packages. "Shirley," one of the most addicted individuals I know, is about the last person anyone would call an addict. She's a successful development director for a great nonprofit that serves the elderly. To look at her, you'd never think Shirley perpetually struggles with substance abuse on a massive scale.

Actually, though, you might think something was going on with Shirley if you did, in fact, look—closely. You might see her red and bloodshot eyes. You might notice how apparently poor is the circulation in her skin. You might realize her posture is off; she's never standing absolutely straight.

Besides being busier than busyness itself, Shirley's addicted to junk food.

"I don't know what to do about it, Steve," she said. "I try to eat better. I try to bring healthy foods to work so I'll grab celery sticks and carrots instead of reaching for jelly beans or a candy bar. But I either forget the vegetables at home or just can't find time to prepare them in the first place.

"It's pretty bad. On my way in, every day, I stop off and get a sweet roll to go with my coffee. Throughout the day, it's all snack foods. And I eat a ton of them, because they never seem to really fill me up."

"You know," I replied, "one thing I could suggest is that you merely slow down a little, Shirley. Eating right does take more time than eating on the go all the time. You do have to shop for and prepare healthy meals. At the rate you're always going, it's not surprising at all that you feel you can't eat right."

We tend to think people this "active" can't be addicts; they don't fit our preconceptions and stereotypes. They're too successful, too productive, too popular. It wasn't until just before she came to see me that Shirley thought of herself as an addict, either. But she was. She'd been addicted to fast food and candy for years.

The addict isn't always the one camped at the transient motel, filling up a syringe and tightening a rubber hose around his arm. It could be the person in the office right next to yours.

It could be the person who works in your office, at your desk.

Habit is as habit does

Habits certainly are unusual. What makes them so unusual is how *usual*—that is to say, how normal—they *seem*. In that way, habits are some of life's trickiest things. They're so hard to distinguish from healthy routines, from actions that are grounded in the cycle of being to which we're all bound.

If you really stop to think about it, what in your life isn't a "habit"? Can't anything you do on a regular basis be considered a habit? Putting on your glasses? Showering? Going to bed? Isn't *eating* a habit?

Dressing, shaving, checking mail, commuting . . . where does an action or behavior stop being something merely regular and healthy and become instead a "habit"?

I think, for this discussion's practical purposes, we should say this: if something you do all the time is good for you, it's a routine. If something you do all the time is bad for you, then it's a habit.

You might, for instance, go out for a walk every morning. While that might be a habit, technically, it's such a *good* one that . . . well, it needs another word to describe it. Though you might indeed be dependent upon taking that walk—even to the degree that if you skip it you become restless and unpleasant—it still doesn't qualify as a habit in the sense of being something you really should stop doing.

Biting your nails is a habit, because it ends up making your hands look like they got stuck in a shredder—because your life (to whatever degree) would improve if you stopped.

Beneficial behavior: not a habit but most likely a routine.

Detrimental behavior: habit.

There it is. A serviceable rule of thumb!

I love coming up with those. It's . . . well, a habit or routine of mine. . . .

The fascinating thing about unhealthy habits is how well they mimic the healthy stuff that each of us, just in the course of being alive, does all the time. This is one reason that, once a habit has a hold, it really sinks its teeth into us; it feels like any one or another of a million daily "items" we never question.

I brush my teeth every day. I never think about it.

I have a cup of coffee every morning. I never think about it.

I know one of those is good for me. I'm not entirely sure about the other.

Habit is as habit does. Take a little time to think about which of your habits are worthwhile—and which aren't.

Then, think about what the ones that aren't are costing you—and whether or not, in the end, they're worth it.

(2) What Addiction Does to Your Life

The slavery of addiction

I asked Tony, an ex-addict whom I met at a New Life Transformation weekend, to write a few words about its slavery.

When you're an addict, you *are* a slave to your addiction. That's really the only word for it. From the moment you wake up in the morning until the moment you finally pass out at night, all you're ever thinking about is how and when and with whom you're going to get high again.

You can even pretend to be going through your daily life, just like anyone else. I did. To look at me from the outside, you never would have thought I was addicted to cocaine. But I was, with every ounce of my being.

I still went to work. Every day I put in a hard day at the office. Heck, in some ways it seemed to me that cocaine helped my work a little. As a salesman, I used cocaine to help me crank up for the big meetings; it got me amped up to get out there and get more clients; it gave me the energy I needed to prepare the best pitches and presentations I could.

At least, I thought all that was true.

It wasn't, of course.

That's just one more lie the addict always tells himself: that the drug is helping him with his life, instead of being honest about the fact that all it's really doing, slowly but surely, is destroying him.

And just as a slave is powerless to prevent the destruction of his own life, so the drug addict is powerless to prevent his drug of "choice" from destroying his or her life.

Being an addict is like being on a crazy, wild train ride you simply can't get off of. At first it seems like an awful lot of fun. You're going so fast! Faster than you've ever gone before! There's all those exciting twists and turns, all the radical, nearly out-of-control ups and downs you experience. All that adrenaline! All that excitement! All that *fun*!

Toot, toot.

Then, after a while, you start to notice that being on that train isn't quite as much fun as when you first climbed aboard. The turns are starting to make you a little sick; the wild highs and lows are making your jaw hurt and your stomach ache.

Now, you *can't* get off the train. It's moving too fast. At a certain point, you're *afraid* of getting off. You're afraid that if you jump off, or pull it all to a stop, you'll find you're now incapable of functioning in the normal world, like it's been so long since you lived off the train that the only choice you really have is to continue "living" on it.

So you just keep shoveling fuel into the engines. If anything, you try to make it go faster, so at least you can try to have as much fun on the ride as before.

At some point on its reckless journey, of course, the train derails. When it does, that is one bad wreck.

I appreciate Steve giving me this opportunity to share a little about the slavery of addiction. I know I said it before, but if you don't mind I'll say it one more time: addiction *is* like slavery.

If you still have a choice, then for God's sake, remain free.

If you don't—if it's too late for you; if you've already been captured—then God help you. No one else can. But God really can, and he wants to use some wonderful people to come alongside you and help you be free again.

The hopelessness of addiction

Julie's a recovering meth addict. Like Tony, through her church Julie heard about and attended a weekend on tranforming your life.

I noticed her right away. She seemed almost pathologically shy; she was someone you sometimes notice specifically because of how hard they seem to be hoping that no one does notice.

As the weekend progressed, she slowly came out of her shell. By the end, she was like the proverbial caterpillar who's now a magnificent butterfly.

Julie's been drug free more than eight years. She's put her life in God's hands, and God has plans for her.

She still knows about the hopelessness of addiction, and I asked her likewise to write for us about it.

I think one of the biggest things about being really and truly hopeless is that you don't realize you're actually in that state. It's like the way a fish probably doesn't realize it's in water; it just *lives* there and isn't aware of any other possible existence.

191

That's the kind of "hopeless" that methamphetamine made me feel, anyway. I couldn't imagine a life outside of one completely dominated by it. All I knew—at *all,* after a while—was that I wanted more meth. That's it. I wasn't thinking about grocery shopping that day. Not about getting another job after my addiction cost me the great job I'd had. Not about fixing anything in my apartment, or getting new shoes, or doing my laundry. Not *showering.* One thing, and one thing only: I was thinking about how and when was I going to get high next.

And in order to get high, I didn't care what I had to do or who I had to do it with. All your standards fly right out the window when getting high is your only concern. When you're very first starting off, it's like a party thing: you do it with people you know, in conditions that are fun; you're just hanging out with friends, having a good time. But that sure isn't how it ends up feeling, at all.

Pretty soon you're hanging out with all kinds of people you wouldn't have dreamed of associating with back when you were straight. Once you become an addict, the kinds of people that once you wouldn't have given the time of day become your new "friends." They become the ones you seek out.

Next thing you know, you're one of the people you used to avoid. You used to look at people who were like the person you've become and wonder how they could possibly live as they do.

Well, now you know. They become drug addicts.

When you're in that condition, hope is the furthest thing away. Hope is for people who still have something in them that's not polluted, that hasn't been blocked out by wretched dependency. Hope is for people who still have reason to believe that for them something better is possible. When you're caught in the grips of addiction, though, you don't think like that at all. You *know* what your future will be. You know how your life is going to go. You know what to expect: nothing.

Tomorrow, and all the days after it, you'll be miserable. You'll have a *little* bit of relief when you get your high (although the pleasure-yield will be less and less), and the rest of the time you'll be trying to get high again. That's it. You know that'll be your life, until you die. That's what the hopelessness of addiction does to you.

But it doesn't have to be that way! Praise the Lord that when you feel like this, drowning in numbing hopelessness, you're *wrong*!

First Peter 1:3–4, under "The Hope of Eternal Life" [in the *New Living Translation*], says this:

> All praise to God, the Father of our Lord Jesus Christ. It is by his great mercy that we have been born again, because God raised Jesus Christ from the dead. Now we live with great expectation, and we have a priceless inheritance—an inheritance that is kept in heaven for you, pure and undefiled, beyond the reach of change and decay.

No one who ever reads those words should *ever* feel hopeless. I read them every day to remind myself of what hope really is and where all hope really comes from.

Praise God, I've been delivered!

(3) How to Give Up Addiction

Honest assessments

The first step of the classic twelve-step recovery program, as published by Alcoholics Anonymous, is this:

> We admitted we were *powerless* over alcohol—that our lives had become unmanageable.

Time and time again, while counseling, I find myself bumping into this exact problem. I cannot help anyone until he first does an honest assessment of his life and admits how out of control of his life he really is.

People *hate* to do that. They do not want to be thought of, even by themselves—*especially* by themselves—as having lost control of their lives. They resist it with all their might.

When they're resisting, there's nothing I can do. If she won't admit she needs help, then you can't give it to her. And that can be *agonizing*. I often feel as if I'm standing on a ship's deck, watching someone drowning directly in the ocean below, and I can toss the life preserver only when she requests it.

"Just *say* it," I feel like I'm screaming. "Just *say* that you're drowning!"

"But I'm not!" she screams back, flailing her arms, going under yet again. "I'm fine! I'm in control! This isn't drowning—it's treading water!"

I hold the lifesaver and wait till she gets just a little more desperate.

If you feel there's any chance at all that you've fallen victim to any addiction, I beg you: *please* do an honest life-assessment.

Talk to people you know and trust; see if there's anything they'd like to say to you about the subject. Think about your life. See if it isn't in more disarray than you've been inclined to acknowledge or accept. Think about your relationships; consider what destructive effects your addictive drives might be having on them.

See if you're not in deeper than you think.

If you are, call 1-800-NEW LIFE (1-800-639-5433). I or one of my friends will be waiting to help.

Seek help!

There are lots of good reasons for any of us to tend toward extreme independence. Primarily, we're just so darned *competent*, aren't we? We know stuff. We get stuff. We're good at stuff. We understand life, and we have a handle on the way life works.

Besides that, we're also usually confident that no one else knows more than we do about any given problem or challenge we're facing. Generally speaking, we're totally right. How could anyone know as

194

much as we do about what we're experiencing? We star in our own shows, and we do know more about what's happening on the middle of our life's "stage" than anyone possibly could by standing in the wings and watching.

Unless that's *us* standing in the wings, watching another's ongoing acts and scenes. *Then* we think *we* have exactly the needed perspective and insight.

(Either way, we're the ones in the know, from our vantage point.)

Just this morning I was listening to some workplace chatter that was happening around a water cooler (seriously). Six or so people were gathered in the hallway outside my office, taking a short break and in search of supportive, friendly conversation.

A woman in the huddle was talking about a personal problem; apparently she isn't too fond of her brother-in-law and is seeing that her perceptible dislike has been starting to cause stress between her and her sister.

What I found noteworthy is that none of the other "conferees" was lacking in advice. Every person in the group had plenty of clarity about what she should say and do—about how she could best go about handling her delicate conflict.

Know what? All the advice was solid.

People really are good at life.

Certainty and confidence, though, readily morph into hubris. If there's one "luxury of personality" that the addict simply cannot afford, it's pride.

If you want to give up an addiction, to regain control of your life, to begin undoing the damage addiction already has done to you and those around you, *you must forgo your pride*. Ditch it. It's doing you no good.

Cling to pride, and your addiction is certain to come along for the ride.

Throw away your pride? Well, then you're free to do the first thing any addict must do before he can start turning his life around: *ask for help*.

You're smart; you're wise; you're capable; you're strong. But you're not powerful enough, on your own, to beat an addiction. For that, you need help.

The *only* way to get help is to seek and request it.

Don't be proud. Ask.

One day at a time

All of us have heard, relative to his struggle to stay clean, that the addict needs to keep himself from relapsing "one day at a time."

This is such a wonderful phrase that I'd like to see it prominently figuring in the lives of *everyone* who pursues spiritual advancement. The truth is, people are too cocky about how powerful they are. So many of us always seem on the cusp of the next big exciting thing that supposedly is going to radically improve our whole life.

It's good to dream. To have goals. To aim high. We all need aspirations and ambitions. At the same time, we mustn't allow our desires for betterment to hide the fact that the life we're leading—today—also needs lots of attention. Where we are needs to matter as much as where we hope to be one day.

I'd argue, in fact, that it needs to matter more.

That's because *God* is with us today. *God* is with us now. God is here, always, in the moment.

Since when isn't God enough?

I think if more people focused on the present, more people would then, necessarily, be focused on God. And if more people were focused on the role and presence of God, right now, I think we'd all have a better life.

Anyone who isn't burdened by the awful weight of addiction has much to learn from those who are. Chief among the lessons to be received is what it truly means to live one day at a time.

The addict, in learning to refocus his attention and care on the actual *is* of today rather than the possible *might-be* of tomorrow, is being brutally authentic about life.

196

Life is about now. If we're honest about life—if we strip it down to its most basic qualities and conditions and live it with integrity—then we must admit and accept that all we have is today.

Today is where the action is. Why would we turn the bulk of our attention elsewhere?

So if you're an addict seeking to give up slavery to gain back freedom, and if you're living "one day at a time," do not allow that in even the slightest way to detract from your self-esteem. It's not just a sign you're working your way out of addiction; it's also a badge of having your priorities straight.

That's *not* a credo to be ashamed of. It's how we all should be living. By *being*, one day at a time, the recovering addict is placing trust and faith in God's fullness. And every Jesus follower is called to do the same.

(4) Gaining Back Your Freedom

Getting to know yourself again

Once more, addiction thoroughly robs you of yourself. The addict lives "the state of being addicted." Can't change what it is, can't modify it into anything else, can't leave it behind in July and come back to it during the winter. If you were an addict Monday, you'll be one Tuesday. You'll be an addict every single day of your life until you fall to your knees and admit that's what you are and nothing else.

Being an addict does nothing if it doesn't steal your identity.

At worst, it goes from being a quality you have to being the only quality you have. First you're "Bob, the salesman with the lovely wife and the two great kids who lives in Boston and always has three drinks at lunch." Then you're "Bob, the salesman who drinks a lot." Then, having lost your job and your family, you're just Bob.

And then you're a homeless guy no one knows.

At "best," addiction to things like cigarettes or sugar won't rob you of your identity as far as others are concerned: everyone in your life may know you merely as someone who chain-smokes or who's forever grazing. Even so, such "acceptable" addictions *do* separate you from the person who, deep down inside, you know yourself really to be. When you're caught in addiction's vise, you are so habitually and severely compromising your core identity that every time you look in the mirror you may as well be wearing a Halloween mask; the person you see reflected is not the you who you know is truly you.

One way or another, addiction is a thief. It's that terrible, and it's that reliable.

However, when you break free, and regain freedom? Then you get to engage in one of the greatest and deepest pleasures life has to offer: reacquainting yourself with you.

The process by which a genuine addiction gradually alters and finally eradicates your sense of identity is slow; it often happens over years of self-abuse. When through God's grace that gorilla gets thrown off your back, you will be *amazed* to discover just how much of you you've been missing!

The world is fresh again.

You are fresh again.

I've never known an addict who's found freedom and wasn't, almost above all, delighted and thrilled by the joy of getting once again to know his or her self. Giving up addiction is like receiving a VIP invite to the most wonderful party anyone ever threw. That celebration is specially thrown to honor you.

Exactly one other guest is there. Jesus.

And oh, what a *time* you two have.

Discovering what was really eating you

Rich had just about everything a man could want. He had an excellent job; he was in terrific health; Sheri, his wife of seven years, was one of the kindest, most beautiful women I've ever met. They had two little children.

About six months after Rich and I became friends, I learned he was having a secret affair. When I confronted him, he told me that even though he knew it was a bad thing, he basically couldn't help it.

It turned out Rich was a serial adulterer.

"I don't know what it is, Steve," he said. "I love my wife. You know I do. And I love my kids; I'd do anything for them. But there's *something* . . . I don't know.

"Sheri likes sex, yes. But not as much as I do, for sure. I don't want to sort of bother her with how much I do like sex, with how often I want it.

"And it's not like she never wants to have sex; she does. Once she's into it, she really enjoys it. I mean, she's not dysfunctional or anything. Bottom line: I can't get the amount of sex from her that I need. So I seek it elsewhere.

"I know I'm not supposed to do that. But I always practice safe sex. Sheri has no idea. We have a happy marriage. This is just one way I keep it happy."

"That's pure nonsense," I said. "You're making up an excuse so you can have your cake and eat it, too. You don't have a happy marriage. You can't. It might seem happy for a while, but it isn't. It's based on a lie; you've made your marriage a lie. Sooner or later, the corrosiveness of that lie is going to destroy the very foundation of your marriage, and you're going to lose it all.

"Sheri, your kids, your house: all of it will be taken away. And all because you think you're such a stud that no one woman can do it for you. You'd better rethink that, Rich. I'm not buying it. Nobody but you would."

Rich actually *heard* me. More than that: he asked me to help him.

I said I would, but only if he promised, that day, to break off the affair he was having and swear to me and to God that he would not start another affair for as long as we were meeting.

Rich made that promise to me, and he pledged to attend the next Every Man's Battle workshop. He humbled himself, and in giving up his addiction to other women, he gained the freedom he needed for the perspective it took to see his dysfunction's root cause.

Rich's father always had affairs behind Rich's mother's back. Though he had no explicit memory of the actions, the fact remained that, through his dad's attitude and choices, Rich had inherited the view that it was admirable, even, to keep a wife at home and have a series of women on the side.

Rich realized what he was doing—ten years ago now. He's never had another affair. Once he had the clarity to see what he actually was doing, he was able, by the grace of God, to finally and fully stop doing it.

The roots of our addictions run deep. But we can't let that deter us from digging as long and hard as we must to once and for all uproot them.

The boldness of accepting a whole new life in Christ

The almost indescribably talented Max was a serious alcoholic until he was about thirty. He wasn't going anywhere; he wasn't doing anything; his whole life barely amounted to a recycling bin's worth of bottles. Today he's one of the most respected artists in the whole American West.

I asked Max if he'd share his story of humbly giving up addiction and courageously accepting a whole new life in Christ.

What I found about being an alcoholic was that I could always maintain just enough of a life to allow me to continue the lie, to myself, that I really had *any* life. I didn't.

I'd been married, but that didn't work out, because the only thing to which I had any real allegiance was the bottle. No relationship I'd ever had amounted to much more than a one-night stand or a dysfunctional, two-person booze-appreciation society.

200

Finally, someone suggested I attend a *New Life Live* weekend on transformation. And that's what changed my life.

Once I realized the depth of my dysfunction, and the terrible rift I'd allowed alcohol to cleave right through the middle of my life, I found myself before God, asking what in the world I was supposed to do now that the cross had replaced the bottle as my life's center of attention. I was ready to go anywhere God led me, to do and be whatever he wanted.

I wasn't expecting God to put on my heart that I should start a theater where only plays pleasing to him would be produced.

Plays! Theater! Acting!

What did I know about these things? Yes, in college I'd done some theater. Yes, I'd always loved live theater; as drunk as I was for as long as I was, I still attended plays. And drunk or not, I'd never lost my respect for the great literature to be found in plays written by the likes of Shakespeare, Ibsen, Shaw, Chekhov, O'Neil.

But actually *starting* a theater company? One that only presented Christian plays?

Was God *kidding*?

Well, I did the only thing I could: I started following exactly where God started leading.

I began talking to people. I started sharing my experience about what God had put on my heart to do.

Slowly but surely, what had at first seemed an absolute impossibility started to take shape.

Today, my theater is one of the most successful year-round repertory theaters in the country. And we still produce only Christian plays.

Trust me: if God lays on your heart that he wants you to abandon your old life and boldly begin a whole new life in him, don't question it. Don't wonder about it. Don't doubt it. Don't argue whether or not it's "reasonable."

It's from God. You don't need any other reason.

Just listen, keep listening, and then take the nudge to connect with some others in recovery.

And prepare, at every step along the way, to be amazed.

(5) Living a Life Filled With Freedom

Discovering how much you've been missing

Dennis is a good man. He loves his wife, and he loves his three children. What he loved even more than them was pot.

I've mentioned before that many folks think marijuana isn't as addictive as some of the other drugs that hook people.

Dennis would be the first to tell you differently. And he would know.

Knowing Dennis's story, I asked if he'd write about giving up addiction, getting back freedom, and discovering how much he'd been missing.

For me, it all broke loose one day when Evelyn sat me down at the kitchen table.

"Dennis," she began. "I'm going to say this to you once, and only once. If you don't hear me, you and I are going to have a serious problem. It's actually reached the point where if you don't change, I'm going to take the kids and leave you."

Right there, that's when my heart sunk into my feet. I knew what she was going to say. And she said it.

"You need to stop smoking pot," she continued. "I've had it. I appreciate that you don't smoke at work, or go to work stoned. But you smoke a joint every night when you come home, and you smoke all weekend.

"When you smoke, you totally withdraw from us. You spend all your time in the rec room watching sports with your friends. And I think that's fine; it's not that I don't want you to have friends. You know I'm not one of those wives.

"But you miss things, Dennis. You miss out on a lot. Tammy had the opening of her school play last weekend, and you were too stoned to go. Bobby had Little League tryouts, and you didn't even know. He had to go out there all by himself.

"All the other little kids had their daddies with them. Bobby's was at home, cradled up with his bong, watching TV. Those are only two of the latest items on a long list of times when our kids needed you, Dennis, and you weren't there. At all.

"That's just the kids. I'm not even going to talk about all the times I needed you, Dennis, and you weren't there, either. The only person you're always making sure to be there for is the guy who sells you weed.

"Well, enough. You either stop, today, or it's over between us."

As much as that hurt me, that was the day I quit smoking pot. I got up from the table, went into my office, and for the first time since I was a kid I got down on my knees and prayed. I prayed hard.

And I felt God in me. And then I knew everything was going to be all right. From there I stood up, collected all my pot and paraphernalia, and got rid of it all. Flushed the weed down the toilet, threw everything else away.

It was over. On that day, I was born again—in two ways.

I was born again to God, and I was born again to my own life.

Today I coach Bobby's baseball and soccer teams, and I'm probably more involved in Tammy's life than she'd like me to be. I learned that, for me, there's no life better than the one that was right under my nose the whole time.

If you've let an addiction rob you of your own life, give up the addiction. And get back to the greatest thing you might not have ever even known you have.

Determining your own fate

Jeff was the graphic designer for a media company in Los Angeles. He did wonderful work, but the truth is, that work wasn't very taxing for him. Jeff was a splendid artist in his own right; years before, he'd had a promising career as a painter.

That was about the time he started to drink. The longer his drinking went on, the more and more comfortable he became forgetting about his own artwork and instead just making a decent enough living creating ad logos and web tiles for his employer.

"It pays the bills," he once told me, shrugging and reaching for another beer. "It's maybe not the most creatively satisfying work around, but, you know. The art world is a tough go. This way, at least my needs are met."

"Are they, though?" I said. I'd finally had enough. "Are your needs really met, Jeff? You're single. Forty-two. Same job for fifteen years. And look!" I pointed to a stunning piece on the wall of his tiny apartment. "*Look* at what you can do. This is the work of an artist, Jeff. You're an *artist*.

"Are you ever really going to be happy if you don't use the gift God gave you? I don't think you will, my friend. I don't think you can be. And I don't think all the alcohol you drink will help you hide from that fact. You need to put down the brews, pick up your brushes, and get your life back."

Though I thought I saw a tear come to his eye, Jeff shooed me with his hand. "Oh, get outta here," he said. "You don't know what you're talking about. I like my life."

Well, he sure didn't like it when, about a month later, he got laid off.

"Steve," he said on the phone, the day after getting the bad news, "could we maybe get together some time for lunch or coffee? I've been thinking about some of the things you said that day in my apartment, about how I'm really an artist. I'm ready to make some changes in my life. But I'm going to need some help with that. Will you help me?"

I don't think I have to tell you what I said.

When I went to see Jeff after that call, I could see he'd already changed. And it wasn't just the Bible on his coffee table that told me Jeff had decided to start walking hand in hand with God. It was also in his eyes.

Jeff put down beer, picked up his brushes, and with God's hand guiding his every stroke, began to paint again.

I got an e-mail this morning from Jeff, now one of the nation's most sought-after artists. One of his paintings has just been selected for purchase and permanent display in one of America's most prestigious art museums.

Through the strength and will of God and the assistance of fellow strugglers, Jeff gave up addiction and got back to the business of determining his own fate. Now, God bless him, he never takes his eyes off the big picture.

Helping others find their freedom

Because of my interest in addiction and recovery, and because of my own recovery, I like to attend groups that are using the twelve-step program. It does my heart well to hear the amazing stories people share about the struggles they've undertaken—and very often still are undertaking—with their addiction to drugs and alcohol.

It's heartbreaking *and* inspiring to listen to those who've become truly humble before God and man tell their tales of failure and triumph. We Christians frequently surround ourselves with those who've already found victory in Jesus, who already know they're saved, who already take continual pleasure in walking with the Savior of all humankind. As gloriously rewarding as it is to spend time in the company of fellow believers, it's also mighty good to be with people at the other end of the journey toward faith, people just now crawling out of the darkness and into the light.

In so many ways, that's where real spiritual transformation is occurring. Not that it isn't constantly taking place in all believers, of course. But the degree of change regularly happening in new believers can be phenomenal.

I go to these meetings, and I sit, and I listen, and what I hear is God. I hear God working in the lives of people who never thought God had any interest in them at all, who maybe never even imagined God existed in the first place. What I hear, time and again, is people being *surprised* by God.

Surprised that he's there. Surprised that he's real. Surprised that he looks lovingly down from heaven and sees even them.

And of all the things that at any given such meeting are deeply inspiring, none is more so than the central principle to the twelve-step program: the assistance—the hands-on help and love—that those further along in the recovery process extend to those newer on the road.

There, addicts help addicts. I can't even describe how astonishing this is to see. The people ten steps up the ladder reach to help those on the sixth rung. The ones on the sixth reach to assist those on the third. Those on the third—people who've often just spent so many years being nothing but a burden that they're moved to tears at being able to be of true value to others—reach to extend their hands to those with one foot still on the ground.

Together, one by one, they all move up.

That's the go-to, let's-do-it model of the Christian life: people who are closer to God helping others move steadily heavenward.

I always show up at these meetings thinking I'll find people who are down on their luck—tough, beaten, defeated. I'm always surprised and humbled to see them exhibiting the true spirit of Christ at least as much as most any other believer I ever meet, on Sunday or otherwise.

Questions for Discussion

1. Do you think there's anything to which you're addicted? Would you be willing to share what that might be, and what deleterious effects you think that has had on your life?

2. Have you ever known a drug addict? If so, what was that experience like for you?

3. What's the hardest thing you've ever had to give up? Why did you have to give that up? What if any lessons about yourself did you learn in the process of giving up the addiction?

4. To what if any degree do you think drug addiction really is just a failure of will on the part of the addict? Do you buy in to "drug addiction as a 'disease'"? Why or why not?

5. If you could say one thing to the worst addict in the world, what would it be?

Conclusion

Giving Up Yourself; Gaining God

I hope this book has inspired you to give your life a long look and to discover things you know you need to change. I certainly understand how unappealing it might be, especially at first, to start self-examining under such a bright light. But I also hope you're seeing that there's no surer way to begin walking from where you are to where you most want to be.

God does want you to experience his best for you. There's just one thing that can ever stop that from happening: you.

You can get in the way. You can interfere with what God's trying to do through and for you. You can insist that what you want to do and how you want to be is bigger and more important than whatever God may have in store.

And, for a long while, you can, in that regard, have it your way. You can do what you want; you can be who you want; you can create for yourself whatever life you think is *it* for you.

God invites you to do that. If you believe you're in a better position than God to decide what kind of life is best, have at it. Create your own life.

Out of his love for you, God will step back and let you do your thing.

When you're done doing that, he'll be there, ready to pick up the pieces.

I am hopeful, though, that going forward there won't *be* pieces for you and God to have to start putting back together. I'm hopeful you'll right your life—that you will remember God, and welcome him front and center—before your life ever reaches the point where God has to come in with a broom and dustpan. I don't want you to hit bottom. I don't want you coming anywhere near the bottom. It's a hard, hard place to be. I know. I've been there.

Instead, it's my hope that you've been moved to seek in your heart and mind evidence of any or all eight symptoms of emotional dysfunction we've addressed, any of which, left unchecked, could well grow into the kinds of weights that start dragging your whole life downward.

Guilt, shame, resentment, fear, anger, instant gratification, help-lessness, isolation, addiction: these throw up massive roadblocks on your journey toward and with God. Just as they can hurt you, though, so can each of them be of immeasurable value to you.

Too often we who believe on Jesus adapt the attitude that, since we walk with him, our every step must be light, perfect, and sure. We don't want anyone to know of our struggles and failures; we fear they might be seen as indications that as Christians we're not as "good" as we should be. So we hide our pain, our insecurities, our concerns that maybe we're missing the mark . . . coming up short . . . not who we're always wanting everyone to think we are.

To a certain extent, that we do this is fine. No one wants to go around airing all dirty laundry all the time, and no one needs to.

What's unhealthy, though, is hiding our "negative" feelings from ourselves. It's extremely easy to do—and extremely dangerous. That's exactly where the emotions and experiences we've discussed become so important.

If you carry guilt and shame, you're in danger of losing your hope.

If you find yourself often feeling much resentment, your ability to love is being threatened.

If fear has come to play too great a role in your life, watch out: increasingly you'll forfeit your ability to trust.

And so on, right down the list.

What we feel, and what we go through, *means* something. "Negative" is only negative if you don't take the time to turn it into a positive. If you feel any of the troubling emotions delineated in this book, or have any of the struggles we've identified, don't dismiss or ignore them. Don't run from them. Don't try to cast them aside as if they're merely proof of your inferiority.

Do the opposite. Run toward them. Dive into them. Believe that God has allowed them in your life because through them he's seeking your attention. They're nothing more than the flipside of a very desirable coin.

You just need to take them seriously.

It's in the unexceptional aspects of your life that you'll find the secrets for starting to live exceptionally. God does want the best for you. He's waiting for you to tell and show him that you want, and will settle for, nothing less.

Stephen Arterburn is founder and chairman of New Life Ministries and host of the nation's number one Christian counseling talk show, *New Life Live!*, heard on more than two hundred radio stations nationwide and on the Family Net and NRB television networks. A nationally known speaker, he has been featured on *The Oprah Winfrey Show*, *ABC World News Tonight*, and *CNN Live* and in the *New York Times*, *US News & World Report*, *Rolling Stone*, and many other media outlets.

Steve founded the Women of Faith conferences and is a bestselling author of more than eighty books, including the multimillion selling *Every Man's Battle* series, *Being Christian*, and *Regret-Free Living*. He has been nominated for numerous writing awards and won three Gold Medallion awards for writing excellence.

Steve and his family live in Fishers, Indiana. He can be reached at SArterburn@NewLife.com.

John Shore, an experienced writer and editor, is the author of *I'm OK—You're Not: The Message We're Sending Nonbelievers and Why We Should Stop*; *Penguins, Pain and the Whole Shebang*; and coauthor of *Comma Sense*, *Midlife Manual for Men*, and *Being Christian*. He also blogs on Crosswalk.com. John and his wife live in San Diego.

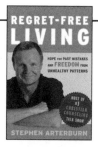
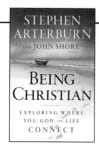

Transforming Lives
Through God's Truth

New Life Ministries is a non profit organization, founded by author and speaker, Stephen Arterburn. Our mission is to identify and compassionately respond to the needs of those seeking healing and restoration through God's truth.

New Life's ministry of healing and transformation includes:

- *A daily call-in radio and TV program, New Life Live!*
- *A nationwide counseling network*
- *Life changing weekend workshops*
    Healing Is a Choice Weekend
    Every Man's Battle
    Lose It for Life Weekend
- *Group Coaching*
- *Treatment for Drug and Alcohol addiction*
- *Books, CDs, Podcasts and others resources*
- *National Call Center manned 365 days a year*

For more information
call 1-800-NEW-LIFE (639-5433) or
visit newlife.com